ADVISORY

D
efinitions
escriptions
ecisions
irections

by

John P. Galassi
Suzanne A. Gulledge
Nancy D. Cox

National Middle School Association
Columbus, Ohio

National Middle School Association
4151 Executive Parkway, Suite 300
Westerville, Ohio 43081
NMSA   **Telephone (800) 528-NMSA**

Second printing August 2001

Sue Swaim, Executive Director

Jeff Ward, Assistant Executive Director, Business Services

John Lounsbury, Senior Editor

Edward Brazee, Associate Editor

Mary Mitchell, Copy Editor/Designer

Marcia Meade, Senior Publications Representative

ISBN: 1-56090-127-6   NMSA Stock Number: 1257

Library of Congress Cataloging-in-Publication Data
Galassi, John P., date
      Advisory: definitions, descriptions, decisions, directions/by
   John P. Galassi, Suzanne A. Gulledge, Nancy D. Cox.
         p. cm.
      Includes bibliographical references (p.).
      ISBN 1-56090-127-6 (pbk.)
      1. Counseling in middle school education--United States
   2. Teacher participation in educational counseling--United States.
      I. Gulledge, Suzanne A. (Suzanne Allen), date. II. Cox, Nancy D.
(Nancy Dailey), date. III. Title.
      LB1620.5.G235   1998
      373.14'046--dc21   98-40525
                                                                        CIP

Contents

About the Authors

John P. Galassi is Professor in the School of Education at the University of North Carolina at Chapel Hill and Associate Director of the Research Triangle Professional Development Schools Partnership. He teaches in the school counseling program and supervises counseling interns at the middle and elementary school levels. In his Professional Development School role, he recently assisted a middle school in revising the goals for its advisory program using the card sort procedure described in this monograph.

Suzanne Allen Gulledge is Associate Professor in the School of Education at the University of North Carolina at Chapel Hill. She teaches courses in middle level education, social studies methods, and social foundations of education. She has co-authored several journal articles and continues to do research and presentations on the topic of middle grades advisor/advisee programs.

Nancy Dailey Cox holds an M.Ed. degree in Middle Grades Education from the University of North Carolina at Chapel Hill. Having taught 6th-9th graders, she understands the importance of making a personal connection with this age group in order to more effectively teach them and to provide needed guidance. With her colleagues, Mrs. Cox sees an advisory program as one tool toward achieving this bond.

Foreword

Was Charles Dickens referring to advisory programs when he wrote, "It was the best of times, it was the worst of times"? Probably not, but the love-hate relationship that middle level educators, parents, and students have with the programs clustered under the advisory label is as strong today as it was in the 1960s and 1970s when thousands of schools added advisory programs, making them a well-recognized component of middle level schools.

While few aspects of middle level schools have remained static, there is little doubt that advisory programs have played essential roles in improving school climate and conditions for young adolescents in those schools. In too many cases, however, the confusion and misunderstanding about advisory programs still persists. This excellent book, *Advisory: Definitions, Descriptions, Decisions, and Directions* is the book we all needed twenty years ago when we tried to determine what advisory programs should be. Fortunately, it is very up-to-date and is needed even more today.

This book lives up to its title and offers a clear and concise explanation of the background information that helps define advisories, describes some essential elements in the design of an advisory program, proposes strategies for planners to use in facilitating decision making, and explores possible future directions and alternative strategies for achieving the goals of advisory programs.

The typology of advisory emphases, in particular, is very helpful in describing six different types of advisories, highlighting the goals and focus skills needed by the advisor, and several sample activities. A card-sorting procedure detailed in the text helps teachers reach consensus on the type of advisory they want and will support.

John P. Galassi, Suzanne A. Gulledge, and Nancy D. Cox are to be commended for preparing this important study of this essential but difficult to implement component of middle schools. In addition to recommending how teachers and students may make current advisory programs more effective, the authors also offer creative suggestions for incorporating advisory into other aspects of the middle school program, through integrated curriculum and as an inherent part of school organization.

— Edward N. Brazee, Editor

Introduction

How can middle school educators be the caring adults who know each of their students well? If one objective of a teacher advisory program is to ensure that each middle schooler be well-known by a concerned professional who is an advocate and advisor for the student, then the decision makers in that school must figure out how to accomplish that objective. This publication proceeds from the premise that advisory programs "are a part of the accepted canon of middle school education" (McEwin, Dickinson, & Jenkins, 1996, p. 75). A previous review revealed extensive variation in the structure and substance of advisory programs (Galassi, Gulledge, & Cox, 1997a). Given the commitment of middle schools to advisory programs and the variety of forms these programs can take, it follows that there is a complex decision-making process that must take place when a teacher advisory program is established or revised.

The central question guiding our consideration of advisory programs is: **How should middle school decision makers go about the process of designing or re-designing their advisory program?** To answer that question this monograph looks at the background information that helps define advisories, describes some essential elements in the design of a program, proposes strategies for planners to use in facilitating decision making, and explores possible future directions and alternative strategies for achieving the goals of advisory programs.

Advisory programs go by various names including advisor-advisee or simply AA, home base, home group, homeroom, the fourth R, teacher-advisor, teacher-based guidance, and locally developed

1

labels such as **PRIDE** and **Primetime**. Such varied programs are almost impossible to define. It appears that whatever a school does and refers to as "advisory" *is* advisory. The lowest common denominator of advisory programs seems to be that they take place at a designated time within the school day with some frequency. Not only are the definitions of advisory programs self-actualizing, they also appear to be evolving over time. In the opening chapter, **Definitions,** we look at the impetus and chronology of advisory programs as well as some well-known manifestations of the concept.

The lowest common denominator of advisory programs seems to be that they take place at a designated time within the school day with some frequency.

Aware of the myriad forms that advisory programs take, in Chapter II, **Descriptions,** we recognize a need for a nomenclature to facilitate discussion about them. Without categorizing these programs by emphases it is difficult to compare and contrast them. Thus we created a typology of program emphases and identified some of their key characteristics. This typology was derived from a review of what middle schools are actually doing in the name of advisories. It displays for planners a variety of options and considerations about structure and procedures. Among the considerations on which we elaborate after presenting the typology are descriptions of obstacles and potential problems that may challenge the success of advisory programs.

Once armed with ample background information derived from the literature, middle school program planners are encouraged to engage in the "hands-on" decision-making process described in Chapter III, **Decisions**. This card-sorting activity enables planners to articulate and compare their preconceived notions about potential goals, activities, and outcomes of an advisory program. The strategy may be used by any number of the developers or constituents of an advisory program, including school personnel, parents, and students.

It is not our intention to be prescriptive, nor to recommend one type of advisory over another. Neither do we intend to suggest that advisory programs are the only way to achieve the goal of assuring that every middle school student is well known by a caring adult in the school. It is for those reasons that we are expansive in the final chapter on **Directions**. We suggest potential venues and strategies in addition to the traditional advisory program approach.

Curricula that address the social and emotional learning needs of young adolescents and respond to the affective as well as the cognitive aspects of schooling may take a variety of forms. We identify, for example, some possibilities described in the context of character education and integrated curricula initiatives. Our aim is to suggest that students' needs for personal/social guidance through adult and peer relationships may be addressed by schools in ways other than what has traditionally been called advisor/advisee. Considering alternative directions should not undermine efforts to create advisory programs, but rather will enhance the processes of planning, collaborative decision making, and creative construction that we believe to be a key to the success of all effective programs. ▲

Chapter I

Definitions

A dvisory programs are defined both by their historical underpinnings and current manifestations. Trends in school administrative structure and curriculum have had significant impact on the nature of AA programs over time, but the conceptual base is easily traced. Advisory programs were specifically developed in response to the need to provide guidance services to students in middle level schools. However the historical roots of the programs were established long, long before the advent of the middle school movement.

Defining advisory programs historically

As a guidance initiative, the history of advisory programs can be traced to American schools in the 1880s (Myrick, Highland, & Highland, 1986). "Vocational and moral guidance" was included as a part of the English curriculum and documented as an innovation by the school principal in a Detroit high school in 1889 (Wittmer, 1993).

As a program specifically for young adolescents, the history of advisory programs is more accurately traced to the early 1890s when it was noted as a feature of junior high schools (e.g., Briggs, 1920; Hieronimus, 1917). Demographic features, including the shift from agrarian to industrial population, in the early years of the century have been identified as contributors to a need for citizenship and character education. Guidance programs in schools were developed in order to provide some common core of preparation of youngsters by their teachers to be good people and good citizens (Cremin, 1961).

In one of the early accounts of a teacher advisor program, Briggs (1920) recounted the experiences of S. O. Rorem, a junior high principal in Sioux City who had published an article about his school in a 1919 issue of *School Review*:

> ...the teacher of each room of the first period in the morning is expected to be the guide, advisor, and friend to whom the pupil may come at any time on any pretext or need....The homeroom teacher is the embodiment of the social, moral, civic and educational guidance. (p. 254)

Briggs (1920) recommended that, "In order that the individual pupil may not be neglected by his several teachers, it has seemed not only wise, but actually imperative, that some adult be appointed as his advisor" (p. 253). His study of 232 junior high schools revealed that 41 did not use advisors, one third used the regular classroom teacher as the advisor, and one-fifth had someone other than the teacher of the pupil as the advisor.

> During the 1920s and 1930s, the role of guidance in education expanded to the point that guidance and education were intertwined.

During the 1920s and 1930s, the role of guidance in education expanded to the point that guidance and education were intertwined. Education was viewed as guidance for living, and the classroom teacher was in a unique position to deliver guidance (Gysbers & Henderson, 1994). Desired changes in behavior rather than prescribed subject mastery was promoted as the objective of teaching. Thus, coverage of subject matter was seen as a means to helping students achieve their purposes and life goals, and homeroom (the junior high predecessor of AA) served an important guidance function.

> The notion that guidance in schools is everybody's responsibility is one that has been voiced repeatedly throughout the years...

The notion that guidance in schools is everybody's responsibility is one that has been voiced repeatedly throughout the years (e.g., Jenkins, 1977; Van Til, Vars, & Lounsbury, 1961) but one which has been emphasized particularly by middle school advocates (e.g., Alexander, Williams, Compton, Hines, & Prescott, 1968; Cole, 1981). Alexander and associates, for example, asserted that the administrative homeroom of the junior high did not provide sufficient guidance and that every teacher needed to be prepared to help students with personal problems and to coordinate the components of their educational programs. The authors proposed the idea of home-based groups led by empathic teacher-counselors skilled in group dynamics, knowledgeable about and able to help students with the developmental tasks of adolescence, and who could supplement the services of counselors by providing personal and educational guidance and related activities in the classroom on a daily basis. Because of their regular contact with students and because of high student-counselor ratios, teachers were viewed as the first source of guidance, and home base or AA was seen as the embodiment of what the old junior high homeroom was intended to be (George & Alexander, 1993; George & Oldaker, 1985).

Defining advisory programs by rationale

As in junior high homeroom programs, the middle school advisory concept recognized that the natural processes of adolescent growth and development worked to create a need for relationships and guidance while prompting severance from supportive contacts and stabilizing influences. "Thus, at a time when youngsters need adult guidance and support the most, they receive it the least" (North Carolina Department of Public Instruction, 1991, p. 11). The challenge for schools was to provide opportunities for adolescents to blossom and to escape from adult domination while at the same time remain under adult guardianship and guidance (Callahan & Clark, 1988).

In recognition of that challenge a fundamental goal of many middle school programs had been articulated. Sometimes referred to as "the fourth *R*," relationship became the focal point of most advisories and was identified as crucial to the middle school concept in general. Van Hoose (1991) asserted that "...the quality of the relationship between teachers and students is the single most important aspect of middle level education" (p. 7). Involvement with a caring and supportive adult and interaction with a small number of peers in advisory period was designed to provide the basis for building relationships in an emotional "home place" within the middle schooler's larger community.

> "...the quality of the relationship between teachers and students is the single most important aspect of middle level education."

Relationships between middle school teachers and their students that emerged when they participated in an advisory group, were characterized as potentially rewarding for both teacher and students. "In many schools with advisory programs, teachers who never thought they could do more than *teach* their subject are learning to provide personal support to students" (Lewis, 1991, p. 33, emphasis added). The mutual benefit notion was a compelling rationale for middle school advisories (Stevenson, 1992). Personal satisfaction, enhanced "with-it-ness," and extension of the teacher's pedagogic and relationship skills were touted as benefits of serving as an advisor.

Myrick (1987) and others have identified working closely with students and building positive relationships with them as important factors in teacher satisfaction and reasons for staying in the profession. Advisees, meanwhile, were to be provided the resources of guidance services that were more immediate than those available from a guidance counselor as well as different from what might be available from parents or other supportive adults.

> Teachers need this type of involvement no less than students do. Since most teachers really do seem to have a deeply felt need to make a significantly positive difference in the lives of their students, and the daily demands of the classroom often seem to make this difficult or impossible, the advisor-advisee program provides the teacher with an opportunity to get to know some manageable number of students in a meaningful way.
>
> (Alexander & George, 1981, p. 90)

In the role of advisor, middle school teachers confronted the affective responsibilities of their profession. While the responsibility for providing guidance had earlier been thrust upon core teachers, there was little done to develop or facilitate the guidance role of teachers before the use of advisories as an integral part of the middle school curriculum. Parkay and Stanford (1992) asserted that an outcome of middle school advisories has been that both teachers and students are enriched by the emotional involvement and guidance service that a teacher provides in advisory programs. They echoed the idea that a good reason to have AA is that it serves particular needs of both adolescents and their teachers, and they noted that there is value in teachers interacting with students in other than traditional student/teacher roles, as is characteristic of middle school AA programs.

> While the responsibility for providing guidance had earlier been thrust upon core teachers, there was little done to develop or facilitate the guidance role of teachers before the establishment of advisories as an integral part of the middle school curriculum.

Middle school advisory programs provide an opportunity for both advisors and advisees to belong to a "family," a chance to secure physical and emotional affiliation without sanctions of grades based on mastery of knowledge or skills. "Since young adolescents need a group to belong to, the advisory time helps students establish positive peer group support, so that they will not have to go outside the school to negative arenas for a sense of belonging" (Ayres, 1994, p. 9). Being involved and interested are qualities emphasized in the advisory group setting. "Grades are not given, discussions are wide ranging or spur-of-the-moment, and student opinion is especially solicited. Teachers and students have more opportunity simply to be themselves" (Arnold, 1991, p. 14). Thus, in what is perhaps its most simple and compelling objective, the advisory would provide a place for individuals to belong just because they are who they are.

When all students belong to an advisory group and there are enough advisors, the groups are sufficiently small so that every student may be well known by an adult. This objective is one that is widely identified in most of the literature on middle schooling in general and endorsed by reports produced by the National Middle School Association (1982; 1995), National Association of Secondary School Principals (1985), and the Carnegie Council on Adolescent Development (1989). Guidance advocates had long called for providing some guidance services by teachers (Gysbers & Henderson, 1994). But the earlier initiatives clearly conceptualized the guidance and advising aspect of the teacher's role as secondary to a basic content-related responsibility. The middle school movement served to elevate developmental guidance to a term of relative importance in the school curriculum.

> The middle school movement served to elevate
> developmental guidance to a term of
> relative importance in the school curriculum.

In time, advisories came to be identified as fundamental to middle school programs because they serve the aims of personal development and social relationship building. They achieved a status almost on par with traditional academic studies. Activities that build school spirit, involve community service, interpret policies and explain procedures of the school, improve study skills, and explore current events are examples of advisory activities that are vital in the middle school curriculum. Middle school advocates believe that the basics are not sufficient if provisions are not also made for students to evolve into self-actualizing persons capable of making decisions, formulating values, relating with others, and recognizing their own self-worth (McEwin, 1981).

> In time, advisories came to be identified as fundamental to
> middle school programs because they serve the aims of
> personal development and social relationship building.

The socialization emphasis of advisories that provides opportunities for communication, not only between teachers and students, but among students themselves in a safe and supportive environment, is important. Providing time to talk and socialize informally is helpful if not essential for students. Muth and Alvermann (1992) include "just plain old-fashioned rap sessions" (p. 7) as a part of advisories while George and Lawrence (1982) specify the importance of effective listening to the talk of advisees by advisors as a strategy for success in an advisory group and as a model for students' behavior toward each other. Communication for the purposes of sharing information as well as for opportunities to practice listening, speaking, and writing skills is an objective typical of most contemporary advisory program descriptions.

Also typical is the rationale that among the special needs of adolescents is the need for guidance as they develop a sense of moral and civic responsibility. Arnold (1991) suggests that advisories should aim to promote students' moral growth and encourage the improvement of those skills that enable young people to function as productive citizens. The development of decision-making skills is often included in this category of objectives for middle school advisory activities.

Students are more likely to feel comfortable discussing such matters of personal concern with a teacher and peers they see frequently in a forum like that provided in an advisory time.

In a typical advisory group, students might be encouraged to articulate both their common and unique problems and together work through some process skills for resolution. Brainstorming, solution webbing, decision trees, and cooperative group problem solving are techniques often used. Advisees might learn coping skills appropriate for their age and situation in a supportive advisory group. Team building exercises and conflict resolution strategies are often practiced in AA periods. Students might consider local, national, and world events and discuss implications of those in terms of their own lives and beliefs. "Ethical questions are welcome for study, contemplation, and resolution. The essence of an ideal advisory is responsible judgment and decision making by students who feel they can safely and candidly discuss issues important to their welfare" (George, Stevenson, Thomason, & Beane, 1992, p. 55).

Students are more likely to feel comfortable discussing such matters of personal concern with a teacher and peers they see frequently in a forum like that provided in an advisory time. "The small advisory group is the place where students can set goals for themselves, make and reflect on decisions, learn more about their own development, and basically enjoy the attention of a caring adult who wants to see them succeed in school" (Erb, 1993, p. 27). The description of the teacher/advisor as the student's advocate is one of the most distinguishing characteristics of middle school advisory programs.

It is clear that the middle school movement extended the notions of guidance programs that existed in junior high homerooms. In addition to the emphasis on "adult for student advocacy" there was "student with student" involvement and subsequent relationship building and also some recognition of the mutual benefit of advisories to both advisor and advisees. Additional objectives, typical of middle school teacher advisory programs, reveal different emphases than school guidance programs historically had included.

The small group setting provided opportunities for developing positive rapport and an attitude of caring, goals many middle schools wished to cultivate. Guidance resources were brought closer to the student population while the scope of the guidance program was enlarged. Referrals for additional services that might be needed by students were facilitated. Students of all ability levels were included in the advisory group, and inclusion was more practical than it might be in core classes. With the advisory program as a fundamental part of the schedule and curriculum of a middle school, its opportunities were made available to every student without regard to levels of achievement and without excluding anyone.

While advisory programs have roots in century-old guidance movements and the junior high initiatives of the early twentieth century, they have evolved to serve broader goals and a more extensive curriculum. Their objectives are aimed at serving both cognitive and affective goals and acknowledging that "guidance is an essential element of effective middle level education" (McEwin, 1981, p. 338).

Our review has broadly identified the following objectives:

- providing opportunities for mutually beneficial interaction between the teacher/advisor and the student/advisee as well as among students themselves,
- promoting social and emotional development,
- encouraging better communication between teachers and students and among students,
- helping improve school morale and spirit by engendering a spirit of belonging and caring,
- providing opportunities for moral and civic growth,
- facilitating guidance services and providing an adult advocate for every student.

These objectives are articulated with varying priorities in a variety of advisory programs.

> While advisory programs have roots in century-old guidance movements and the junior high initiatives of the early twentieth century, they have evolved to serve broader goals and a more extensive curriculum.

Defining advisory programs by outcomes

An in-depth review of the literature concerning the outcomes or effectiveness of advisory programs is beyond the scope of this monograph and is available elsewhere (Galassi et al., 1997a). Only a summary of findings is included here.

First, however, a few general considerations must be stated. To date, we are not aware of any systematic program of outcome research on middle school advisory programs. Research in this area is limited to one-shot investigations. Some of this research is unpublished (Connors, 1986; Doda, 1979 reported in George & Alexander, 1993; Nathaniel & Damico, 1979 reported in George & Alexander, 1993) which makes it difficult to evaluate the adequacy of the methodology and the validity of the conclusions. We are only aware of six published studies which directly address the outcome question with middle school students (Espe, 1993; Mac Iver & Epstein, 1991; Putbrese, 1989; Sardo-Brown & Shetlar, 1994; Totten & Nielson, 1994; Ziegler &

Mulhall, 1994). Most of these studies have serious methodological flaws which compromise our confidence in their conclusions (see Galassi et al., 1997a). For example, the components of the advisory programs they studied varied considerably, and this fact makes generalization across studies difficult. Bearing these limitations in mind, what follows is a summary of the findings for middle school advisory programs as judged by students, teachers, principals, and parents. These findings should be considered tentative at best.

With respect to impact on students, the findings are:

(1) The programs may improve teacher-student relationships. The majority of students perceived the advisor as someone in whom they can confide or feel comfortable in approaching about a concern at school (Espe, 1993; Totten & Nielson, 1994), although perhaps not about a personal problem (Zielger & Mulhall, 1994).

(2) Although it is difficult to know whether the results are due to different program emphases and/or different developmental needs of the students, older middle school students may derive different benefits from advisory programs than younger students and may be less positive toward these programs (Sardo-Brown & Shetlar, 1994; Totten & Nielson, 1994). In the Totten and Nielson study, the majority of the sixth graders indicated that the program helped them set goals and become more responsible; whereas, the majority of seventh graders said that the program helped them to work out problems with other people. Seventh graders were somewhat less positive toward the program and perceived less recognition in the program than sixth graders. Seventh and eighth graders in the Sardo-Brown and Shetlar study felt that advisory was a place to do homework and take a break; whereas sixth graders felt that the purpose was to take a break followed by socializing and doing homework.

(3) Advisory programs may have a more positive impact on girls than boys (Putbrese, 1989).

(4) These programs may benefit students in other ways. Putbrese (1989) reported that advisory programs (a) gave students a feeling of more control over decisions, (b), promoted an atmosphere of equality, (c) improved the sharing of feelings between students, and (d) reduced the incidence of smoking and/or alcohol use.

The literature also suggests that advisory programs have a number of beneficial effects as judged by teachers.

(1) Teachers either felt the program is necessary (Sardo-Brown & Shetlar , 1994) or has value (Espe, 1993; Ziegler & Mulhall, 1994), liked serving as advisors, felt good about their work with advisees, and believed that student behavior in class had improved, students were more cooperative, and that students felt more a part of the school than before (Ziegler & Mulhall, 1994).

(2) Teachers perceived the advisory program as reducing class absences and tardies, especially over a three year as compared to a one year period (Ziegler & Mulhall, 1994). Whether actual rather than perceived reductions were achieved is unclear from the study.

(3) Teachers who served as advisors felt that students confided in them and sought academic advice from them (Espe, 1993).

Beneficial effects as reported by parents were suggested in two studies.

(1) A majority of parents felt that the advisory group was a good idea. They felt they knew who their child's advisor was and had talked to the advisor. Moreover, they felt that they understood report cards better, knew more about their child's progress, and found it easier to stay in touch with teachers. In addition, their perceptions were somewhat

more positive three years after program implementation than one year after (Ziegler & Mulhall, 1994).

(2) A majority of parents in a school with an advisory program (a) agreed that their child's transition into the secondary school had been made easier by the program and that the advisor was actually looking after their child and (b) saw the advisor as the person to contact regarding questions at school (Espe, 1993).

Only one study reported effects for middle school advisory programs as perceived by principals. In a national survey, Mac Iver and Epstein (1991) reported that, even after family and student variables, region, and grade reorganization of the school were controlled statistically, principals with strong advisory programs reported that they had stronger overall guidance programs and estimated lower high school dropout rates for their middle school students. Unfortunately, no data about the relation between these estimates and actual dropout rates was provided.

Regardless of the perspective of the participants studied, the limited existing research does suggest positive effects for advisory programs.

In summary, regardless of the perspective of the participants studied, the limited existing research does suggest positive effects for advisory programs. Once again, the reader is cautioned about the tentative nature of these conclusions as the enduring effects of advisory programs are unknown at this time when judged from an empirical research perspective. 𝔸

Chapter II
Descriptions

Advisory programs carry myriad objectives. For example:

1. Provide an environment and activities that will foster bonding with an advisory group so that students will feel accepted and valued by teachers and peers.
2. Help students cope with academic concerns and set goals that will facilitate positive school experiences.
3. Give students avenues to discover their uniqueness so that they might come to appreciate the many differences among people.
4. Help students develop positive relationships through experiences that utilize group dynamics.
5. Promote critical thinking skills through discussion and problem-solving activities so that students can learn to make responsible choices.
6. Develop listening skills and an understanding of the roadblocks that hinder effective communication.
7. Build self-esteem in students so that they might become confident, capable young people who accept responsibility for their own actions.
8. Heighten student awareness of good citizenship through providing opportunities for meaningful contributions to their school and community.
9. Provide opportunities for extensive student involvement through shared decision making.

10. Improve home/school communication and relationships.

(Hoversten, Doda, & Lounsbury, 1991, p. 6)

The list is representative of the variety of objectives that may be incorporated in these advisory programs. Activities may be as seemingly disconnected as intramural sports, DEAR (Drop Everything and Read), and routine administrative announcements. In fact, almost any type of activity that one can think of or devise could be included because no universally accepted definition of these programs currently exists. Given this diversity, it is difficult to discuss advisory programs as a single conceptual entity and also misleading to do so as two advisories may differ greatly in terms of their objectives and/or activities.

> It is difficult to discuss advisory programs as a single conceptual entity and also misleading to do so as two advisories may differ greatly in terms of their objectives and/or activities.

An advisory typology

In examining advisory programs, however, we found that, although they frequently overlapped, we could differentiate them with respect to the type of need they primarily address. Different needs are associated, to some extent, with different program emphases, curriculum (program activities), advisory roles/skills, and structural organization. Some programs, for example, emphasize affective needs of students; whereas, other programs seem more concerned with needs in the cognitive area. Moreover, we found that these distinctions are conceptually useful with respect to planning advisory programs, comparing different programs, and understanding a number of the problems these programs subsequently encounter.

Table 1 provides an advisory typology we devised and have found to be a helpful guide for advisory practice and research (Galassi et al., 1997b). The typology focuses on the *primary* need the program is designed to serve with secondary consideration being given to advisor role and skills, the focus of the program, time demands, and the

Table 1: A Typology of Advisory Emphases

Type	Need	Time	Goals & Focus	Advisor Skills	Sample Activities
Advocacy	Affective	Substantial implementation time	Adult-student relationship	Personal qualities — interest and concern for students	Individual student conferences
Community	Affective	Substantial implementation time	Group identity	Personal qualities — group management	Group discussions, projects, intramurals
Skills	Affective and cognitive	Substantial "prep" and implementation time	Developmental guidance	Personal qualities — group management, group facilitation	Decision making, stress management, race relations, values clarification
Invigoration	Affective	Minimal "prep" time	Relaxing, recharging	Personal qualities, enthusiasm	Intramurals and clubs, parties, informal "fun" activities
Academic	Cognitive	Substantial implementation time	Academic performance	Personal qualities, teaching	Study skills, silent reading, writing, tutoring
Administrative	Administrative	Minimal "prep" and implementation time	General school business, "housekeeping"	Clerical, organizational	Announcements, distributing school materials, collecting money

nature of the curriculum (activities). It permits comparison among different programs, enables us to clarify our conversations about what advisory is and informs our research. Specifically, we propose six advisory types or emphases based on the conceptual need identified: Advocacy, Community, Skills, Invigoration, Academic , and Administrative.

The first cell of the typology specifies the particular emphasis of the advisory program. Advocacy-type AA programs emphasize the personal relationships between the teacher and student. Moving down the chart we identify other types of AA programs. Community-oriented programs focus on group dynamics, morale building, and social relationships. Skills programs emphasize developmental guidance and life skills for adolescents in both cognitive and affective realms. Invigoration programs provide a period for disconnecting from the formalities of the academic program with time to "unwind" or "recharge one's batteries" so that the student might be refreshed and better able to resume academic instruction. The last two types have aims that are less associated with the affective realm. Academic programs emphasize cognitive skills associated with content area learning and might include monitoring and improvement of students' grades and study skills labs. The final program type is classified as Administrative as it accommodates the usual "housekeeping" tasks of school announcements, money collection, and similar tasks. A brief description of each type of program follows considering the issues of what aims to serve, what amounts of time and advisor skills are required, and what sort of activities might be included.

"...the psychosocial characteristics of middle school students can baffle not only students themselves but also their teachers and parents."

Adolescents need adult support and guidance to function at optimum levels but "the psychosocial characteristics of middle school students can baffle not only students themselves but also their teachers and parents" (Watson, 1997, p. 2). Advisor/Advisee programs identified as the **Advocacy** type are those that aim to attend to students' individual needs by providing time and opportunity for a concerned adult in the school to get to know them well. For example, in advocacy programs such as the Shoreham-Wading River Middle School Advisory Program (Burkhardt & Fusco, 1990; Shoreham-Wading River Middle School, 1989), the relationship between the teacher and the individual student is paramount. Although group activities may be used, individual conferences and informal meetings are stressed as ways to engender comfortable relationships as a student talks with an advisor about personal concerns. The advisor must get to know each student personally in order to serve as a student's advocate. Having only a small number of students assigned to each advisor and generous amounts of time with them are obviously important factors in the success of advocacy-type programs. Teaming or cooperating with another responsible adult in the school would make it possible for the remainder of the advisees to be involved so that a conference between an advisor and an individual advisee could occur. Of course, there are other ways for a student and advisor to get to know one another well, but in most schools with limited time in the instructional day and high student-to-faculty ratios, it is a challenge to engender close and supportive relationships that adequately serve individual students. Availability of guidance services and collaborating with guidance counselors is likely to be an integral part of a successful program that places primary emphasis on advocacy needs.

> Availability of guidance services and collaborating with guidance counselors is likely to be an integral part of a successful program that places primary emphasis on advocacy needs.

Community type programs serve what may be referred to as social or belonging needs. The transition to middle school, when students leave established and familiar environments at a particularly vulnerable developmental stage, has been identified as a stressful period for young adolescents. Young adolescents need an environment that assures them they belong, that they have a place where they "fit in" and are important to a group (Eccles, Wigfield, Midgley, Reuman, Mac Iver, & Feldlaufer, 1993). Community-oriented advisory programs recognize that middle school students may feel a sense of alienation. Young adolescents, especially sixth graders, lose the security of the elementary school classroom where they came to know both their teacher and peers well; middle schools tend to be larger than the schools that feed into them and students have contact with both a larger number of classmates and teachers each day. To combat the social and physical anonymity that can result, faculty and staff attempt to build relationships within small peer groups. The name "homebase" is particularly appropriate for this advisory type. Before implementing such programs, teachers and parents must be carefully prepared, fully informed, and involved.

The role of the advisor in the community type AA program is one of fostering a sense of belonging to a "school family." Emphasis focuses on building a group identity through such activities as selecting an AA name and song, creating a motto or logo, engaging in friendly competition with other advisory groups, completing a community service project, and engaging in intramural games. Significant amounts of time and advisor input are required to plan and implement consensus building, manage conflict, and sustain group identity in this type of advisory group.

> The developmental guidance approach recognizes that each individual is unique but progresses through some common growth stages with related needs.

There are similar resource requirements as well as some shared aims in the Community type and the next type of advisory program. However, because an additional need is addressed, we distinguish the third type of program, **Skills**. Many schools recognize the value of using the AA period as a vehicle for delivering a developmental guidance program. The developmental guidance approach recognizes that each individual is unique but progresses through some common growth stages with related needs. Advisory time is used to address the issues that arise out of these stages. Regarding the curriculum, Myrick (1993) lists eight possible unit topics:

1. understanding the school environment,
2. understanding self and others,

3. understanding attitudes and behaviors,

4. decision making and problem solving,

5. interpersonal skills and communication skills,

6. school success skills,

7. career awareness and educational planning, and

8. community pride and involvement.

The guidance lessons are structured and include objectives and anticipated outcomes such as: students will understand the relationship between academics and future success; students will demonstrate ways of coping/getting along with others (Myrick, 1993).

This type of program requires the most staff development. The input of students and developing a comfortable peer relationship in the advisory group is valuable in this program, but is not so much the main focus of the curriculum as it is in the Community type previously described. The role of the adult leader in the Skills type program is especially significant. Although that person is not necessarily subsuming the role of the guidance counselor, she is expected to demonstrate skills such as active listening and group discussion facilitation that are typically part of the training of counselors.

Next on the advisory program chart is the **Invigoration** type. Although it is similar to the Skills type in terms of requiring a particular set of abilities and dispositions of the advisor, it differs from the Skills type in terms of what is to be accomplished and dispositions needed to succeed. Just as we recognize the value of recess in an elementary school setting, many schools feel the need for a "time-out" from the more intense academic program. Invigoration time provides a setting for informal interactions among students and between staff and students. These programs provide an opportunity for students (and advisors) to have fun, to recover from "mental fatigue," and/or "blow off steam" before resuming instruction. The physical and psychological changes that adolescents go through can result in restlessness, limited attention span, irritability, and aggression or physical impulsivity that can fluctuate with changing activities. "Teachers of adolescents can also expect more conflict if they are not willing or able to allow students to have some independence or control in the classroom" (Meece, 1997, p. 92).

Invigoration time provides a setting for informal interactions among students and between staff and students.

The advisor's role is to maintain a balance between pandemonium and constructive activity. Personal attributes and skills of advisors are important factors in this regard. If students are to be invigorated by having some control over their activities during this type of advisory program, then a structured curriculum for the period is not essential, and planning and implementation time and resources differ from those required in the types previously described.

Logistically, an Invigoration program may accommodate larger groups. However, there is a potential liability that comes with the great flexibility of this advisory type. Planners should take into account the possibility that parents will disparagingly consider it "free time." Questions regarding the ability and intent of staff to interact at this level of informality are also relevant considerations. Nevertheless, it may be that Invigoration programs have a greater chance for success with both students and teachers. Research by George and Bushnell (1993) provides a list of activities that students deem fun and are advocated for use by advisors. These include: celebrating birthdays, recognizing holidays, discussing common problems and concerns, completing service projects, and playing games. Students like deciding for themselves and having control over activities. With respect to the teachers' favorite activities, they list student of the day/week, organization day, goal day, career talks by adults from the community, silent reading and writing, joke and riddle day, clubs, and intramurals. Many of these enjoyable activities require a minimum of teacher preparation.

The next type is the **Academic** advisory. These programs are designed primarily to meet cognitive educational needs that can be distinguished from the affective realm. The major goal is academic enhancement, and thus activities such as Drop Everything and Read (DEAR) and study skills builders provide the primary content. These programs do not require as much additional training in counselor-type skills so necessary in Skills programs. Programs with academic emphases might be especially attractive in communities with a strong academic orientation or as a transition step toward a more affectively oriented AA (White & Greenwood, 1991). In such a program, the advisor moves a step outside of the more familiar role of content specialist and assumes that of advisor. An effective advisor/advisee program requires that students and teacher work together outside their normal content-specific relationship. Study skills activities can provide the basis for building new types of relationships. Small groups of students assigned to one teacher for one or more years may meet daily for a time period sufficient to teach and practice the skills. The authors define the study skill type activities as going beyond the "how to(s)" and including lessons such as goal setting, self-observation, and assessment of behavior.

Programs with academic emphases might be especially attractive in communities with a strong academic orientation or as a transition step toward a more affectively oriented AA.

One other program type, **Administrative**, may also facilitate some affective program goals though it is not established primarily for that purpose. Serving in a familiar role, teachers communicate school information to a group of students. Common tasks such as taking attendance, reading the daily bulletin, passing out school materials, and collecting lunch money are typical activities in Administrative AA programs. The major purpose is completion of a variety of "housekeeping" tasks, although relationships between teacher and students or among students may be strengthened during this time as well. The activities in an Administrative homeroom program are specific and purposeful, related to tasks that are essential to the smooth running of the school. Little teacher preparation time is required and tasks do not generally require additional staff development. On those days when there is little or no school business to transact, the advisor may be challenged to fill allotted time with meaningful and engaging activities.

Administrative homeroom type advisories, like each of the other five we have identified, are not as discrete and distinct as their appearance in the typology. Yet, the six different emphases in advisory programs we have identified, based on the type of needs they are designed to meet, stand up to the test of application to some well-known advisory program curriculum packages. A wide variety of AA goals and activities can be accommodated by the classifications of the typology. The process of considering existing programs in light of the typology can be an instructive exercise and helpful in the task of comparing and contrasting programs.

> The six different emphases in advisory programs we have identified, based on the type of needs they are designed to meet, stand up to the test of application to some well-known advisory program curriculum packages.

Obstacles to advisory programs

In designing a teacher advisory program, there are a variety of potential obstacles to be addressed by planners. Surveys of existing programs and interviews with those who direct them (e.g. Cawelti, 1988; Epstein & Mac Iver, 1990; Myrick et al., 1986; Valentine, Clark, Irvin, Keefe, & Melton, 1993) suggest some common and recurring problems. These collected cautions about potential stumbling blocks for advisory programs need to be classified and considered along with suggestions for avoiding them. We propose a conceptual framework for identifying potential barriers to achieving successful advisory programs and suggest that they can arise at any of the phases in the life of a program – planning, implementation, or maintenance .

The rush to implement an advisory program, especially when prototype programs are available in packaged form as kits, is a time when the need for extensive deliberation and planning may be overlooked. Several barriers to advisories arise in the incipient phase of program planning. We call these *conceptualization barriers*. Essentially they are goal-setting, staff development, and job description issues that can become obstacles if not attended to carefully. They are encountered when (a) planners fail to identify or agree on the needs of the school community the program will address; (b) the staff have, or perceive themselves to have, inadequate skills to implement the program; or (c) insufficient consideration is given to how the advisory program will affect the advisor's existing workload.

Obstacles take on a variety of forms in the context of the phases of program development.

Obstacles take on a variety of forms in the context of the phases of program development. After a program moves past the conceptualization phase, another set of impediments may be encountered. These are *implementation* and *maintenance* barriers. They consist of inadequate resources in any of the following areas: planning, staff development, time in the school schedule for the program, interesting activities, or support for the advisory program among parents or other key stakeholders.

Conceptualization barriers are the first hurdles encountered, as planners try to identify and articulate what needs can be addressed by an advisory program. Eichhorn (1996) suggests that the planners' first question must be about the function of the program. Before selecting a program to follow, even one that is known to have worked well in another school, it is important that a careful and deliberate process of goal setting be undertaken to determine locally appropriate and supported functions for advisories.

As noted earlier, the purposes that advisories may serve are so numerous that the biggest task may be to identify a primary need or a manageable cluster of needs to be met by the program. The advisory typology may be useful as a point of reference for program designers as they attempt to identify advisory functions they can agree upon and those that can realistically be addressed at their school. Failure to confront this issue may prove to be an obstacle at a later time when planning has resulted in activities that some constituents of the program do not find useful. For example, major problems can occur later if key stakeholders such as parents, administrators, or influential subgroups of teachers do not agree on the need(s) to be addressed by the program. Thus, if an affective focus is selected, and activities in AA reflect that orientation instead of academic skill building which some members of the school community endorse, the program may come under attack and perhaps be derailed at a later time. Another obstacle can be the temptation to identify too many goals in an early effort to satisfy everyone at the planning stage. Problems with implementation and serving well the identified goals are inevitable if the advisory program promises to do more than it is equipped to do. The program is likely to result in fragmented efforts that fail to achieve much of anything and end up frustrating everyone involved.

The next consideration is, what skills will be required of those who staff the program? The premise, fundamental to advisories, that guidance is everybody's responsibility can be problematic at the outset. Every faculty and staff member, not just classroom teachers, but administrators, guidance, and resource professionals may be involved if the desired adult/student ratio is to be achieved. Many staff members may not accept advising as one of their responsibilities, and even those who do accept may feel unprepared to fulfill the guidance responsibilities. Many middle school teachers, particularly those who were initially prepared at the secondary level, see themselves as content specialists and often do not feel comfortable with such counseling-like skills as group facilitation. Moreover, research has demonstrated repeatedly that adequacy of preparation for the advisory role is a continuing concern of teachers (Cole, 1994; Hutcheson & Moeller, 1995; Scales & McEwin, 1994).

Every faculty and staff member, not just classroom teachers but administrators, guidance, and resource professionals, may be involved if the desired adult/student ratio is to be achieved.

The third potential barrier that should be considered during a program's inception is the current workload of the potential advisors. How much will the program under consideration add to that workload? Over the years, teachers have been assigned an ever-increasing number and range of responsibilities. New duties get added, while old ones are rarely dropped. Advisory programs represent still one more time-consuming responsibility to many teachers and, time may be of special concern to teachers who lack the necessary skills and who have not been trained for the middle grades. Indeed, in some instances the concern has been so pronounced that teachers have filed grievances over the addition of teacher-based guidance to their duties (Ames & Miller, 1994). Thus, the following issues should be addressed at an advisory program's inception: (a) how much time and preparation the program will add to a teacher's workload, (b) whether other responsibilities can be dropped or scaled back to compensate, and (c) whether, in teachers' opinions, the potential gains from the program appear to justify the required efforts. In addition, a teacher's perception of what tasks comprise his or her role as a teacher may become a focal point when that teacher is called on to be an advisor. That teacher may feel that an expectation to fill a new role has been imposed. And, if the teacher's propensity is to resist change, then the issue becomes a conceptualization barrier to the advisory initiative.

> Attention to conceptualization and planning, even if
> it means delaying the start of a program, is an
> oft-repeated caveat of experienced AA leaders.

Attention to conceptualization and planning, even if it means delaying the start of a program, is an oft-repeated caveat of experienced AA leaders. The conceptualization barriers need not be insurmountable, although they can represent formidable obstacles for advisory programs. Awareness is the first step in overcoming them, while giving sufficient attention to them is next. Efforts devoted to identifying and agreeing on the needs to be met by a program, specifying the skills required of advisors in the program, and addressing work load commitments prior to initiating the program are important measures to take to avoid the pre-implementation barriers that could undermine the program in later phases.

Although many later phase problems can be averted at the outset, a budding AA program can be compromised if activating and sustaining efforts are not carried out deliberately and effectively. Obstacles that present themselves at the implementation and maintenance stages perhaps pose a greater challenge simply because they continue to exist as potential problems for as long as the program is in place. Important resources – time for planning and staff development; a regular and sufficient time allotment for the program; interesting activities; teachers who are favorably disposed toward advising; and parent, administrator, and counselor support – may be available one moment and disappear the next. A closer look at these potential barriers will illuminate some inherent problems.

Implementation and maintenance of an advisor-advisee program in a school is likely to involve ongoing encounters with lack of time for planning and revising the program and teachers' negative attitudes toward the task. One teacher reported that the thought of having to plan for an extra period, the need to revise the school schedule, the lack of curriculum materials and resources, and eventually feelings of frustration, discontent, and disruption caused the program to be abandoned after four years (Hart, 1995).

Finding the time for actually scheduling the advisory period is always a major concern.

A number of advisory program proponents have stressed the importance of intensive and extended planning and staff development not only prior to, but also during the implementation of an advisory program (e.g., Ames & Miller, 1994; Ayres, 1994; Gill & Read, 1990). The nature of what is done with the time allocated for planning is likely to change between the inception and implementation phases. Once a school begins actually having advisory time, the needs of students and their rather unpredictable reactions to what is going on may require revisions in plans. In addition, during the implementation stage advisors may need training in skills such as responding to students' feelings, clarifying or summarizing ideas, asking open-ended questions, complimenting and confronting, linking feelings and ideas, setting limits, and acknowledging contributions (Wittmer & Myrick, 1989). The value and usefulness of these skills may become apparent to advisors only as they become involved with students and their real needs.

Finding the time for scheduling the advisory period is always a major concern. It is easy to judge how important a program is thought to be by looking at the place it is given in the master schedule. Brief (less than 20 minutes) or infrequent advisory periods reveal something about the importance of an advisory program in a school's curriculum. A related issue is determining whether the time is being used in the way that it was intended. At the implementation and maintenance phases, an ongoing effort of those who oversee and administer the program should be concerned with tracking how advisory time is actually used.

The way that time is used during advisory periods is related in some degree to the resources that are available to advisors. Although numerous guidelines and activity books for advisory programs exist, the lack of availability of these resources is a common obstacle to building a successful advisory program. At the same time, excessive reliance on an overly structured set of advisory activities represents a major advisory obstacle for other teachers and students. Developing advisory activities that sustain the interest of both students and teachers is a challenging task dealt with in the next chapter.

> **Excessive reliance on an overly structured set of advisory activities represents a major advisory obstacle for other teachers and students.**

Middle school principals, teachers, and counselors bear the responsibility for implementing advisory programs but also the burden of keeping them working successfully. Principals, for example, can provide much more than simple administrative support in the form of materials, supplies, and a scheduled time free of interruptions. "The understanding and support of the principal is the key determiner of success or failure" (McEwin, 1981, p. 345). There is a generally held belief that the top-down effect of a principal's lack of enthusiasm for advisory time will negatively influence teachers and undermine the program. Moreover, data reported in a NASSP survey by Valentine and associates (1993) indicated that, although a majority of middle grades principals attributed importance to advisory programs in middle schools, a majority did not plan to implement them.

> There is a generally held belief that the top-down effect
> of a principal's lack of enthusiasm for advisory time will
> negatively influence teachers and undermine the program.

Obviously, teachers are vital to the success of advisories. Cole (1994) asserts: "The teacher is the key to a successful teacher advisory program. If teachers in a school do not embrace the program, it will fail" (p. 3). In addition to specific skills, a critical factor for teachers may be one of an affective quality; lacking that attitude will prove to be a major obstacle to success. That attitude or quality may be characterized as caring or child-centeredness. It is an inclination to be constructivist in approaches to curriculum design and in building relationships through activities that are interesting and meaningful to both advisors and students. Most teachers want their experiences in classrooms to be creative and integrative for themselves and their students, characterized by self-motivated learning and decision making; but the conditions that nurture those qualities are often nonexistent in traditional paradigms of schooling (Brooks & Brooks, 1993).

The people involved as constituents, including school personnel, must be considered as potential resources as well as potential obstacles to success of an advisory program. The school counselor is commonly identified as an important resource and the coordinator of an advisory program.

> The people involved as constituents, including
> school personnel, must be considered as potential resources
> as well as potential obstacles to success of an advisory program.

Parents are potential obstacles to the success of advisory programs. Sometimes parents who never experienced an advisory program when they were in school, do not understand such programs, resist the idea of time being taken from core subject classes, and may even resent the suggestion that their children need a program designed to help them build relationships and get help with personal and social needs. There exists a general public suspicion of "non-academic" activities in schools, and those suspicions may undermine advisory programs. To achieve and maintain parental support for advisory programs, therefore, is an ongoing responsibility.

In summary, the reasons why some advisories fail and others succeed are complex. Often the obstacles to initiating and maintaining successful programs change over time and barriers overcome return as roadblocks. It is difficult to plan, implement, and subsequently maintain an advisory program. This is a clear reality. Yet the value of quality advisories continues to be advocated by middle school educators, and the need to provide students with the sort of guidance that advisories promise appears to be increasingly pressing (Gill & Read, 1990).

The literature that describes advisory programs that have encountered and overcome obstacles is instructive and should be considered as a part of the planning, implementation, and maintenance of future programs. In the next chapter, **Decisions**, the choices that need to be made in planning and revising advisory programs are discussed. Ⓐ

Chapter III
Decisions

As discussed in the previous chapter, the particular emphasis chosen as a primary focus for your advisory program plays a major role with respect to a variety of issues such as skills advisors need, the type of activities required, and others. However, it is neither the only factor nor does it determine the specific decisions to be made. Our approach to making program decisions is not prescriptive because there is no accepted basis for determining best practices. Rather we recommend taking into account the implications of both the program emphasis that has been adopted and the knowledge/suggestions gleaned from the research and clinical experience literature on advisory programs. The discussion that follows summarizes the advisory literature for a number of important decision areas, but is by no means exhaustive.

Does your middle school need/want a freestanding advisory program?

This question may strike the reader as either rhetorical or heretical. After all, a freestanding advisory program has repeatedly been identified as one of the ten essential elements of a "true" middle school (NMSA, 1982), and an adult advocate for every student is one of the six general characteristics of developmentally responsive middle level schools (NMSA, 1995). Moreover, 93% of 130 reputedly exemplary middle schools included advisory programs (George & Oldaker, 1985), and, in a 1993 study of 1,798 middle schools, 52% of 6-8 grade schools and 47% of all the schools, including grades 5 to 9, had a teacher-based guidance (advisory) program (McEwin et al., 1996). At the same time, advisory is frequently viewed as:

... both the most popular component of the curriculum of middle-level schools and the most disliked. Ironically, it is sometimes the most valuable use of the school day and at other times a nearly complete waste of everyone's time. It is often the program most attractive to some parents and the most offensive to others. (George, 1986, p. 184)

Thus, we view the question as fundamental and essential. We encourage the reader to reflect on the issues raised in this chapter as well as the alternatives to a freestanding advisory program discussed in Chapter 4, **Direction**s, before answering the question.

If school decision makers conclude that an advisory program is needed, then a variety of questions must be answered beginning with the needs to be served and the emphasis of the program.

Determining program emphasis: A card-sorting approach

If school decision makers conclude that an advisory program is needed, then a variety of questions must be answered beginning with the needs to be served and the emphasis of the program. Previously we have identified six different emphases that an advisory program can have and discussed the implications of these emphases for advisor skills and activities. How does an advisory planning team determine the extent to which important stakeholders share a common perspective about the needs and goals of the program? Without agreement, support for the program can erode over time as different priorities surface and come into conflict.

We have devised a simple card-sorting task to facilitate achieving consensus on program emphases. The Appendix (p. 78) contains 24 numbered statements which characterize an advisory program and may be cut out and pasted on 3 X 5 index cards. The first four statements (#1, 7, 13, 19) characterize advisory programs that emphasize individual advocacy or a one-to-one caring relationship between the advisor and each student. The next four statements (#2, 8, 14, 20) are characteristic of programs that focus on developing a sense of community in the advisory group. Similarly, there are four statements for each of the other program emphases: skills or developmental guidance [#3, 9, 15, 21], invigoration [#4, 10, 16, 22], academic [#5, 11, 17, 23], and administrative [#6, 12, 18, 24].

Individuals administering or making decisions about the program are presented with the cards and given the following instructions:

> The cards given to you each contain a statement which can be especially characteristic of or emphasized in an advisory program. It is impossible for an advisory program to contain each of these 24 characteristics or emphases, so we have to make choices or set priorities. The choices we make are very important because they reflect the needs and goals we believe to be most important to a middle school student's development. Hence we need to examine our fundamental beliefs about middle school students and advisory programs in making these choices.
>
> You are asked to set priorities for the program by sorting these 24 cards into three piles. The **first pile** should contain the statements that are the most important or the **highest priority** for the advisory program as far as you are concerned. It should contain four and only **four cards**. The **second pile** should contain the next most important or the **next highest priority** statements, and it should contain four and only **four cards**. The **third pile** should contain statements of the **lowest priority** and should contain **16 cards**. Some of the goals on the cards are similar to each other, and selecting more than one of these cards indicates that you place a high priority on that type of goal for your program.
>
> Once you have completed your sorting write the numbers of the cards you placed in piles one and two (high-

est and next highest priority) on the **Summary** card in
the appropriate spaces. Please return the summary card
and all other cards to the person who is facilitating this
exercise.[1]

One effective way of using the card-sorting task is to have advisors from each grade level sort the cards individually. Advisors at
different grade levels may envision different program emphases for
middle school students. Sortings by individual advisors enable each
advisor to be explicit and concrete about advisory preferences. By
comparing the card numbers with the goal categories (e.g., cards #1,
7, 13, 19 are consistent with an advocacy emphasis; cards #2, 8, 14, 20
are consistent with an emphasis on community), the advisory emphasis for each teacher can be determined.

Team sorting allows the members to discuss their
preferences and to come to consensus as a team.

Once the individual sortings have been completed, sorting can
be completed by each middle school team by grade level. Each team
would be given only the cards that each of its members had individually sorted into the highest or next highest priority categories. In this
instance, sorting would be done by the team collectively. Team sorting allows the members to discuss their preferences and to come to
consensus as a team. Once again the cards would be sorted into three
piles – highest priority (four cards), next highest priority (four cards),
and lowest priority (16 or fewer cards depending on how many had
been eliminated for a team as a result of the previous sorting by the
individual advisors for that team). Each team would then summarize
its sortings on the summary card. Comparing the numbered cards
chosen with the advisory goals (i.e., advocacy, community, and others) yields the relative advisory emphasis preferred by each team.

---

[1]In using the card sorting task, note that the number of cards (4) assigned to
each of the first two piles is not entirely arbitrary and enables one to determine whether all the cards in a pile represent a similar program emphasis
(e.g. advocacy) as the pack of cards contains four cards for each of the six
emphases.

One final sorting remains – sorting the cards across the teams for each grade level. Prior to this sorting, however, it is helpful for a facilitator to provide some conceptual information about the six different types of program emphases (advocacy, community, skills, invigoration, academic, and administrative) so that advisors also have a conceptual framework in addition to their personal priorities on which to base their sorting. Thus, for example, advisors would be told about the emphases of an advocacy-oriented advisory program and which of the 24 statements were characteristic of it. In this final sorting, they would also be asked to consider how much they thought they could effectively accomplish in their advisory program. Armed with this background, the advisors for each grade would be given only the cards which the teams for that grade level had previously sorted into the highest and next highest priority categories (advisors may have the option to reconsider previously discarded cards if they desire). Each grade level would then sort the cards into three piles – highest priority (four cards), next highest priority (four cards), and lowest priority (16 or fewer cards depending on how many had been eliminated as a result of the previous sortings by individuals and teams for that grade level). During this sorting, it is useful to have a facilitator who helps guide the discussion and assists the advisors in their efforts to reach consensus on the priorities for the advisory program for that grade level. Once again, the priorities for each grade level are written on the summary card and inspected to determine the desired emphasis for the advisory program.

The priorities can then be reviewed and discussed at a subsequent meeting. Some important discussion questions include the following: *To what extent is there commonality across grade levels in advisory program priorities? If little commonality exists, how comfortable and supportive is the faculty and other interested parties in having different advisory program emphases at different levels?* The card-sorting tasks and the discussions that follow substantially increase the likelihood that a faculty and other stakeholders will reach consensus about the fundamental needs and goals of the advisory program and that they will subsequently support the program.

The same card-sorting task could also be completed by a sample of students at each of the different grade levels in order to determine the extent that their priorities are similar to those of the advisors. In this case, however, only a single (individual) sorting would be completed by the students. Their sortings could then be examined in order to determine the percentage of times that each of the six types of advisory goals (advocacy, community, skills, invigoration, academic, administrative) was chosen. Those percentages would indicate the type of emphasis that students prefer for the program. Similarly, the sorting could also be completed by a school administrator, a school governance committee, and by a sample of parents as a means of resolving disagreement about the needs to be served by the program and building consensus for it. Discussions among the major stakeholders could then be conducted in order to reach consensus on the goals for the program.

> Obtaining parents' support for an advisory program, and especially one that attempts to meet affective needs of students, is especially important.

Obtaining parents' support for an advisory program, and especially one that attempts to meet affective needs of students, is especially important. A number of parents oppose advisory, homebase classes, and school counseling programs on the grounds that they take time away from critical academic subjects and/or because they are seen as involving children's feelings about personal or private family matters (Kaplan, 1997). According to Kaplan, these parents view topics such as self-awareness, decision making, acceptance of individual differences, and so forth as interfering with parents' or religious leaders' ability to determine values as well as right and wrong in these areas. In many instances, they perceive the values presented about these topics in advisory as being in direct contradiction to those taught in the home.

Optimum size of advisory groups and optimum meeting time
There is no clear consensus among experts as to the ideal num-

ber of students for an advisory group. Generally, however, educators favor advisory groups that are small, less than typical class size. Determining the size of the advisory group depends on the number of available advisors. Smaller advisory groups (12-18) are possible if there is a large number of advisors. The program emphasis is also a factor. An advisory emphasis on advocacy and strong one-to-one relations with advisees calls for fewer advisees. On the other hand, an invigoration advisory emphasis that relies heavily on intramurals permits a higher advisee/advisor ratio.

With respect to the best time of day to schedule the advisory period, the virtues of beginning the school day with advisory in order to get the day off to a positive start are frequently touted. On the other hand, scheduling it before or after lunch or at the end of the day may give the perception that advisory is not on par with regular classes. A strong argument can be made for beginning instruction as the first activity in the school day and saving advisory until fatigue occurs and then using the advisory period as a way to re-invigorate both students and advisors.

Frequency and length of advisory

The most current information about frequency and length of advisory periods is provided by McEwin, Dickinson, and Jenkins (1996), who surveyed 1,798 middle schools (grades 5-9) in 1993. These researchers found that the most prevalent practice by far is scheduling daily meetings, with 63% of all middle schools surveyed reporting this pattern. The next most frequent pattern is just once per week, reported by 14% of the schools surveyed.

There were four categories of period length used in this study: 1-15 minutes, 16-30, 31-45, and more than 45 minutes. The most common advisory period length reported was 16-30 minutes by 65% of the schools. One to 15 minutes and 31-45 minutes tied for the next most common length period with 15% of the schools reporting periods in these ranges.

Length of advisory period would also seem to be influenced by program emphasis. An administrative focus, for example, would seem to fit comfortably in the 1-15 minute time period, whereas an invigoration program that stressed intramurals might work better with a 31-45 minute period. Similarly, frequency of meetings might also be affected by program emphasis. Although an invigoration program might profit from a longer advisory period, it may not need to meet as frequently as other types of programs.

Who should be advisors and what characteristics should they possess?

Once again there are a number of factors to consider in this decision. Current practice indicates that *all* professional staff serve as advisors in 56% of the schools surveyed (McEwin et al., 1996). With respect to staff other than classroom teachers, resource teachers (56%), counselors (39%), media specialists (36%), and administrators (27%) most commonly served as advisors in all schools surveyed with similar percentages in evidence for 6-8 schools (McEwin et al., 1996).

Should students be paired with advisors with whom they would not ordinarily have as teachers during a typical day? To our knowledge, there are no empirical data to help answer this question. An argument in favor of such pairings is that the student is not being graded by such individuals and therefore can relate more easily and naturally without fear that what is revealed to an advisor will adversely affect grades. On the other hand, it can be argued that students more naturally form relationships with the adults with whom they have the most frequent contact. Thus, if students see an adult only in an advisory period, they are less likely and less able to confide in this person than if they had contact with that adult at other times of the day as well.

There are some advisor characteristics and behaviors that are desirable regardless of program emphasis. Bushnell and George (1993) reported five characteristics of effective advisors: (1) They care about the students in their advisory group and demonstrate that care in a variety of ways; (2) they are able to relate to the individuality of various advisees; (3) they are available to their advisees; (4) they have a positive attitude toward advisement, and (5) they have their own unique styles of advisement. The authors noted that males were particularly concerned about having advisors who respected their opinions and joked with them, while females wanted advisors who cared about what happened to them at school and were available to talk. The obvious implication of these findings is that, if mandatory participation of all staff is not required in order to produce advisory groups of manageable size, then selection of potential advisors might be based in part on these characteristics.

Other advisory research studies yield contradictory suggestions and clearly are a function of the perspective of the research participant. For example, 15 nationally recognized experts in middle level education recommended that advisors remain with their advisees for the duration of the student's enrollment in that school (Gill & Read, 1990); whereas, middle school students in one study preferred that the advisor be changed each year (Sardo-Brown & Shetlar, 1994). Not surprisingly, students stated that they should be able to choose their own advisor, while teachers did not believe that students should choose their advisor (Sardo-Brown & Shetlar, 1994).

Multi-age advisories and length of the advisor-advisee relationship

Two empirical studies about the effects of multi-age advisories were identified. The Espe study (1993) was conducted with students in grades 8-10, and therefore it is difficult to know how applicable it is to younger adolescents. The participants in Ziegler and Mulhall's (1994) study, however, were 6-8 grade students. The majority of these students liked the cross-grade advisory groups and felt they provided a good opportunity for meeting and knowing others, discussing topics that don't come up in regular classes, and for strengthening positive feelings between advisors and advisees. Also students showed an increase in sense of belonging and feelings of being involved in decision making after three years of the program as compared to after only one year.

On the one hand, including students from all grades appears to have the advantage of developing a general sense of the middle school as a total community rather than a sense of community within grade levels. On the other hand, some educators suggest that the activities and needs of middle school students vary with grade level, a condition that supports single grade advisory programs.

We do not know of any empirical data about the effects of maintaining the same advisor for the middle school years versus changing advisors each year. An argument for maintaining the same advisor-advisee relationship over a student's middle school career is based on the premise that the relationship will get stronger and closer over time. On the other hand, a personality mismatch between an advisor-advisee that is allowed to endure throughout the student's middle school years completely contradicts the purposes of an advisory program.

> A personality mismatch between an advisor-advisee that is allowed to endure throughout the student's middle school years completely contradicts the purposes of an advisory program.

What role should the school counselor play in an advisory program?

An advisory program is a form of teacher-based guidance, and as guidance is the professional specialization of the school counselor, counselors often assume a leadership role in the advisory program. What is the best role for a school counselor to play in an advisory program? The following is an abbreviated discussion of a topic that we have addressed elsewhere (Galassi & Gulledge, 1997).

Middle school counselors may play several different roles in teacher-advisor programs. In some instances, these roles overlap, but each undoubtedly has advantages and limitations, and in planning or revising an advisory program it is important to consider each of the possible roles.

The most obvious role is that of a direct service provider, that is, being one of the advisors. Since guidance is everybody's responsibility and participation by all school personnel will ensure advisory groups of manageable size, the counselor functions as one of the many advisors and implements the same activities as other advisors (Johnson

& Salmon, 1979). An advantage of this approach is that counselors and teachers relate on common ground; a disadvantage is that it makes limited use of the counselor's special training and expertise.

As an "expert" the counselor may serve as the advisor for those advisees who are less responsive to teacher-based guidance or who have special needs such as racial awareness and violence reduction (Myrick, 1993; Myrick & Myrick, 1990). The assumption is that the counselor's special training enables her/him to reach these advisees more effectively. The counselor may use advisory activities, small group counseling, individual counseling, or other interventions to help these students. In other cases, the counselor's role is to be available during advisory time to see special referrals from other advisors.

Another very logical role is to have the counselor serve as consultant for the program. In this role, the counselor functions as a resource teacher, working with advisors who are having difficulty and providing or developing advisory activities and curriculum materials for the advisees. In the latter capacity the counselor serves as the central resource person to gather, design, and distribute advisory materials. The strength of this role is that it allows for wider dissemination of counselors' special expertise and enables them to work with a larger number of teachers, thereby impacting a larger number of students.

Training and supervision, some of the most widely advocated roles for counselors in advisory programs, also involve widespread dissemination of the counselor's expertise. They are among the most beneficial contributions by counselors as teachers tend to resist advising because they feel ill-prepared to implement it. Fortunately, research studies indicate that in-service training enhances teacher readiness to conduct advisory programs.

In-service training typically focuses on active listening and other basic counseling techniques and on skills to facilitate interaction in small groups. It also should be tailored to the particular program emphases that have been adopted. Once an advisory program is implemented, training may have a more situational focus or a supervisory component. A counselor might co-lead or model an occasional advisory session, especially for teachers who experience difficulty with their advisory groups or evaluate the success or failure of an individual faculty member's efforts to implement the program.

Finally, a number of authors have proposed that counselors assume the central leadership or coordinating role in advisory programs. Henderson and La Forge (1989), for example, proposed advisory as a service sponsored by the guidance department for which the counselor is the designer, coordinator, and consultant. The counselor's primary tasks are assessing a school's readiness for advisory, forming a teacher advisory committee with the counselor as the chairperson, and preparing faculty to serve as advisors by training them in communication skills such as reflecting feelings, clarifying, universalizing, linking, summarizing, focusing, giving information, and blocking.

Other proposed counselor leadership functions include helping the faculty develop a rationale and common approach or philosophy for advisory, acquainting new faculty with program goals, orienting students to the program, serving as a public spokesperson, overcoming resistance from students, teachers, and parents, and evaluating the program.

The role of leader/coordinator is certainly one that the counselor is well qualified to assume, but it may not always be an ideal one. If "'teachers are the heart of a school's guidance program" (Myrick, 1993, p. 61) as well as the major service providers, then their perspectives should be a principal consideration in those programs. Teachers may be more receptive to advisement programs when the committee is led by one of their own (Ayres, 1994). Moreover, teachers frequently believe that counselors and principals will plan programs that teachers will find difficult to maintain. Because of the importance of program ownership to long term success, it may be advantageous for the counselor to serve as a resource person and facilitator to an advisory committee which is chaired by a teacher and composed of teachers, with additional representation from administrators, parents, and students (see Gill & Read, 1990). Such a committee may be more likely to design a program that will achieve broad-based teacher and community support.

Given the varied suggestions of writers, it is impossible to be prescriptive about the "correct" role for a school counselor in an advisory program. Clearly, it is advantageous for the counselor to be involved, but which role should be adopted is probably best determined by considering the advantages and limitations of the possible roles with respect to the particular school situation.

Given the varied suggestions of writers, it is impossible to be prescriptive about the "correct" role for a school counselor in an advisory program.

Should incentives be provided for advising?

A variety of factors are involved in explaining why teachers are often less than enthusiastic about participating in advisory programs. Lack of pre-service preparation is one factor. But time is also an important consideration. In an era of decreasing resources, demands to accomplish more with less, and a seemingly ever-expanding list of teacher duties and responsibilities, the amount of teacher time an advisory program requires is no small issue. It is an especially important one in a school where consideration is being given to adding the program on top of teachers' current workloads. Moreover, for teachers who were trained in secondary rather than middle school education, an advisory program is frequently perceived as not only one more responsibility but one they may not feel is an important one. Available data also reflect this teacher time concern. Cole's (1994) study of middle school teachers attending an AA preparation workshop revealed that 36% of them had ambivalent or negative feelings about being an advisor and one of their major reservations was time – time to plan the program, the time that advisory supplants other curriculum, and time for one more lesson and one more lesson plan. A reluctant teaching staff who lacks program ownership is a major obstacle to a successful advisory initiative (Gill & Read, 1990). Thus, the issue of how much time an advisory program will add to a teacher's workload, whether other responsibilities can be dropped or scaled back to compensate, and whether, in teachers' opinions, the potential gains from the program appear to justify the required efforts represent important issues to address.

A reluctant teaching staff who lacks program ownership
is a major obstacle to a successful advisory initiative.

Still another consideration is whether to provide financial or other incentives either for serving as an advisor or for demonstrating excellence in advising. Modest annual stipends might be provided for individuals who serve as advisors, and/or financial or other awards could be instituted to recognize excellence in advising. Many people would argue that it is not appropriate to provide extra compensation to teachers to perform a function that is a legitimate part of their job. However, the commonly held perception that advisory programs represent yet one more duty for teachers does reduce teacher support for those programs. As such, temporary artificial incentives may need to be provided to support enthusiastic participation in advisory until sufficient numbers of teachers are imbued with middle school philosophy and have adequate training to serve as effective advisors.

Training and planning considerations

Is special training needed for teacher-based guidance? If so, how much and what kind? "Ironically, there is probably more staff development required for an effectively functioning advisor-advisee program than any other aspect of the middle school" (George & Alexander, 1993, p. 225). As discussed earlier, studies indicate that teachers, especially those not trained in middle grades education, feel inadequately prepared to serve as advisors. Moreover, even those trained specifically for middle grades education often feel inadequately prepared for the advising role. A study by Scales and McEwin (1994) surveyed graduates from programs in five states that contain 57% of all undergraduate middle level preparation programs in the country and found that 73% rated their preparation for advising to be less than adequate. Although not currently the norm, middle level preservice teachers need to be prepared to handle advisory roles and work with experienced classroom teachers who are involved in advisory programs. Fortunately, however, research also suggests that in-service training significantly enhances middle-grade teachers' readiness to conduct advisory programs (Myrick et al., 1986). In addition, the provision of staff development prior to implementing advisory programs does appear to be the norm. Although the details of the training (e.g., length, content) were not provided, McEwin and associates (1996) reported that 82% of all the middle schools surveyed engaged in staff development prior to initiating their programs.

> Clearly, the initial training should be tailored
> to the particular program emphasis selected with its
> requisite skills or advisor personal characteristics.

Clearly, the initial training should be tailored to the particular program emphasis selected with its requisite skills or advisor personal characteristics. Thus, choosing a skills development program emphasis, for example, would dictate that advisors receive training in basic counseling skills such as active listening, small group facilitation and management, and others. In addition to training prior to the program, periodic supervision and occasional booster training and sharing sessions are very important once the program is initiated. Such sessions are widely recommended and provide advisors an opportunity to hone and refine their skills and to confront and collectively resolve advisory problems as they are experienced. Moreover, the value and usefulness of advisory skills become especially salient to advisors as they become involved with students and their real and continuing needs over time. Ayres (1994), for example, recommends periodic in-service activities for teachers coupled with support and encouragement for at least the first three years of the program. Assuming that skilled school counselors are available on staff and can function in a training role, little or no extra cost would be incurred for this training and support.

Substantial planning time is essential when a new advisory program is to be implemented effectively. Estimates of the amount of time needed to plan and initiate a full program for a middle school range from a minimum of six months to upwards of two years or more (Bergmann & Baxter, 1983; Cole, 1994; Goldberg, 1977; Hertzog, 1992; Ziegler & Mulhall, 1994). A number of major tasks need to be completed during the period including deciding on the needs/goals to be served by the program and the program emphasis; publicizing and obtaining active support for the program from teachers, administrators, parents, and students; making decisions about the program details (e.g., activities, frequency and length of meetings); and providing effective in-service preparation. Many of these tasks can be spearheaded by a broad-based advisory committee consisting of teacher, administrator, counselor, parent, and student representatives. Moreover, it would be advisable for the committee's deliberations and decisions to be well-publicized and reviewed in meetings open to all interested stakeholders.

> Estimates of the amount of time needed to plan and initiate a full program for a middle school range from a minimum of six months to upwards of two years or more.

What activities should be included in the program?

In making decisions in this area, a number of factors must be examined including program emphasis, student considerations, teacher needs, and demands on teacher time.

As stressed earlier, the particular emphases of the advisory program are a major influence on other advisory decisions, including the type of activities recommended. The typical activities in a program that emphasizes academic enhancement, for example, will be considerably different from one emphasizing invigoration. At this time, we are not aware of any articles or books that categorize advisory activities according to the program emphasis they are intended to serve. Nevertheless, it seems imperative in selecting activities for program planners to consider the extent to which the activity appears to further the intended program emphasis. Of course, many activities may be compatible with more than one type of emphasis. For example, intramurals seem relevant to both invigoration and community emphases. In general, however, an assessment of whether intended activities appear to further the chosen program emphasis seems advisable.

There are also several student factors that merit consideration in choosing advisory activities. First, the literature and experiences with advisories suggest that students prefer activities that are fun, less structured, stimulating, relevant to their own lives, and over which they can exercise some degree of choice (e. g., George & Alexander, 1993; Sardo-Brown & Shetlar, 1994; Totten & Nielson, 1994). Research by George and Bushnell (1993), for example, provides a list of activities that students deem fun and are advocated for use by advisors. These include celebrating birthdays, recognizing holidays, discussing everyday problems and concerns, engaging in service projects, playing games.

The opportunity to exercise some choice in the selection of activities is a factor in students' attitudes toward them. Relevant to these findings, Glasser has consistently maintained that students work harder and are happier in environments where they are able to satisfy their basic needs – survival, belonging, power (sense of importance, of stature, of being considered by others), freedom, and fun (e.g., Glasser, 1992). The advisory group potentially satisfies students' belonging and power needs, while the specific advisory activities can address the basic needs for fun and freedom, with the latter being satisfied through the exercise of freedom of choice by students in helping to determine the activities to be used. An important implication of these findings is that many students probably prefer the activities associated with an invigoration program emphasis as opposed to some of the other emphases in which adults are likely to make most of the program decisions.

In selecting advisory activities, it is also advisable to be aware of possible developmental differences that might impact advisory programs for sixth, seventh, and eighth grade students.

In selecting advisory activities, it is also advisable to be aware of possible developmental differences that might impact advisory programs for sixth, seventh, and eighth grade students. Totten and

Nielson (1994) found that seventh graders were less excited about an advisory program than sixth graders. Sardo-Brown and Shetlar (1994) reported that seventh and eighth graders felt that advisory was a place to do homework and take a break; whereas sixth graders felt that the purpose was to take a break followed by socializing and doing homework. Thus, student needs may vary as a function of grade level, and, accordingly, the emphasis of the advisory program and the choice of activities for sixth, seventh, and eighth grade programs may need to differ as well.

Student needs also vary as a function of culture and gender differences, but advisory programs are designed to reach all students. According to Banks (1994),1990 census data revealed that one of every four Americans is a person of color. Moreover, it is projected that one of every three Americans will be a person of color by the turn of the century (Commission on Minority Participation, 1988) and that students of color will account for 46% of the school-aged children by 2020 (Pallas, Natriello, & McDill, 1989). These projections suggest that it is critical for students to learn to understand and appreciate diversity if our society is to function effectively. Understanding and appreciating people who are different from ourselves is a frequent goal of advisory programs. But people's ability to appreciate, value, or even tolerate others is affected by their own levels of self-esteem (Aronson, 1997; Slonim, 1991).

Enhancing students' positive feelings about themselves is another important goal of advisory programs and middle grades education itself. However, the identity and self-esteem issues of minority and non-minority youth are clearly not the same. Gay (1994) asserted that a clarified ethnic identity is central to the psycho-social well-being and educational success of youth of color. Achieving a clarified ethnic identity for an African American student, for example involves being able to "...negotiate simultaneously in three realms of experience: the mainstream, the African-rooted Black culture, and the status of an oppressed minority" (Boykin in Gay, 1994, p. 152). Gay proposed four principles that can assist with this process: (1) exploratory learning; (2) creating caring and supportive learning environments;

(3) facilitating the personal development of students; and (4) implementing developmentally appropriate instructional strategies. A number of these principles can and are frequently incorporated in advisory programs, and some unpublished research cited by George and Alexander (1993) suggested that African American students may be more responsive to their advisors than white students.

> While assisting middle school minority students with
> identity and other developmental needs in advisory programs,
> advisors must simultaneously help non-minority students
> address their own identity needs as well as issues of
> tolerance of others and respect for diversity.

While assisting middle school minority students with identity and other developmental needs in advisory programs, advisors must simultaneously help non-minority students address their own identity needs as well as issues of tolerance of others and respect for diversity. Wardle (1997), for example, proposed an anti-bias and ecological approach to multicultural education that seems relevant to consider when selecting advisory activities. It involves teaching students about seven factors – race, culture, gender, disability, family, community, and socio-economic status – which affect their sense of identity. The strength of this approach, according to Wardle, is that the child rather than the culture is the focus and that it "...recognizes that children experience integrated contexts, not a series of distinct, opposing factors" (p. 152).

Spring (1995) presented another suggestion that appears to have merit in helping students accept and appreciate themselves and others while simultaneously addressing the needs of both black and white middle grade students. He cited the need to provide models of white antiracist activities as a means to minimize white guilt, defensiveness, and psychological escape behavior by white students and expressions of hostility by black students when racial issues are discussed. Spring's recommendation takes on special importance given the finding that racial cleavage in friendship patterns increases from the elementary to the secondary school years, making interracial friendships increasingly rare during adolescence (DuBois & Hirsch, 1990).

Writing about racial identity in racially mixed schools, Tatum (1997) noted how educators are frequently concerned about how often students group themselves with others of the same race. She suggested that when time is unstructured, for example at lunch or play, students should not be coerced into social groups to achieve racial or ethnic integration. In a subsequent interview (O'Neil, 1997), she suggested that it is important to create opportunities for students to have discussions and non-competitive interactions in un-tracked, racially integrated settings where there can be cross-racial dialogue. Advisory time might be used to provide that sort of opportunity in a school.

Finally, Swick, Boutte, and Van Scoy (1997) assert that there are four essential components to promote:

1. nurturing authentic and positive self-esteem;
2. promoting a sharing, nurturing, and positive self-other relationship syndrome;
3. nurturing the cultural strengths of all people, and
4. promoting collaborative relationships among different cultures. (p. 119)

Once again, many of these components are incorporated in advisory programs. But how does an advisor nurture the cultural strengths of all people? A key factor appears to be how these are dealt with in an advisory curriculum. Are they simply included and "touched upon" in the curriculum from the mainstream cultural perspective, or is the curriculum transformed to treat an issue from multiple and equally valid cultural perspectives (Banks, 1994, 1995; Gay, 1997)?

> ...teach the perspectives of the mainstream culture (don't assume students already know them); teach the perspectives of other cultures (with the message: they're equally valid to some); and examine similarities and differences between cultures...*both* similarities and differences should be addressed so that your students move from

merely tolerating differences to viewing them as accept-
able, desirable, and valuable.... (Sanchez, 1997, p. 161)

Sanchez also cautions against a trivialized "tourist" curriculum
emphasizing that a diversity curriculum goes beyond holidays and
foods. Although it may include these, it involves developing an understanding of the values, viewpoints, and traditions that characterize other cultural groups.

After a three-year study of successful teachers of African American students, Gloria Ladson-Billings (1994) described those teachers
as engaging in culturally-relevant pedagogy. Their approach to teaching was characterized as consistently equitable and respectful of students. Teacher relationships with students nurtured socio-political
consciousness. The exemplary teachers of African American students
described by Ladson-Billings provided opportunities for students to
investigate and discuss the cultural norms, values, mores, and insti-
tutions that produce social inequities. To prepare students for active
citizenship, she found programs such as a middle school community
problem class to be helpful.

**Other studies suggest that middle school boys and girls
have different educational experiences and needs; they
may respond favorably to different advisor characteristics.**

Other studies suggest that middle school boys and girls have
different educational experiences and needs; they may respond favorably to different advisor characteristics. With respect to the former,
Roberts, Sarigiani, Petersen, and Newman (1990) found that the relationship between achievement and self-image was more positive for
sixth grade boys than for sixth grade girls. In addition, the relationship tended to increase for boys and for girls as they moved through
middle school. Spring (1995) summarized a number of findings by
Myra and David Sadker indicating that boys and girls in the same
classrooms have very different educational experiences. Among their
findings are the following:

(a) girls were equal to or ahead of boys on most measures of achievement and psychological health in the early years of schooling, but had fallen behind boys by the end of high school;

(b) boys receive more and better instruction than girls;

(c) teachers are more likely to call upon boys to answer questions than girls, interact more with boys than girls, and spend more time answering a boy's question than a girl's question;

(d) women are not as well represented in textbooks as men; and

(e) girls suffer a greater decline in self-esteem from elementary school to high school than boys (31 percentage points vs. 20).

Given their dissimilar educational experiences, Bushnell and George's (1993) finding that girls wanted advisors who cared about what happened to them at school and were available to talk is not surprising. Boys, on the other hand, wanted advisors who joked with them and respected their opinions. Thus, advisors may serve different functions for girls and boys. They may help girls cope with the inequity they experience in school and the accompanying emotions engendered; advisors may have more of a social and a validation function for boys.

> Exploring gender roles and how cultures define them and deciding for themselves what roles they will adopt are part of the maturing process for adolescents.

Havighurst (1972) identified the developmental task of achieving a masculine or feminine social/sexual role as one that adolescents need to address. Among the appropriate activities for advisory programs in response to that adolescent need might be to consider how gender and sex roles are reevaluated and reinterpreted in contemporary society as a way of helping students come to terms with those roles. Exploring gender roles and how cultures define them and deciding for themselves what roles they will adopt are part of the maturing process for adolescents (Rice, 1998).

With respect to teacher needs for advisory activities, findings from the research literature appear to be contradictory at first glance. On the one hand, a study by Zielger and Mulhall (1994) suggests that teachers wanted more resources in the form of guidebooks or lesson plans that would provide "structure and content to depend on" (p. 45), while Sardo-Brown and Shetlar (1994) reported that a majority of teachers in their survey wanted a less structured advisory program and wanted to do away with the packaged lesson plans purchased for the program. Teachers' preferences for advisory materials probably are related to their preparation and experience with advisory programs as well as the time demands they experience. Thus, teachers with limited preparation and background for the advising role and/or with limited preparation time would be expected to prefer and depend on the perceived security of well-defined and structured advisory handbooks. On the other hand, teachers who have more experience and more time to prepare would be expected to welcome the opportunity to tailor advisory activities to the unique needs of their students. In addition, it may be part of the typical developmental process of moving from initial reliance on a structured advisory curriculum as one gains experience and matures as an advisor to preferring a much more individualized and free-flowing advisory program.

Regardless of experience level, a host of resources are available, including both well known advisory curricula such as PRIME TIME (1985) and FAME (1984) and handbooks created by local school districts. One excellent source book is *Treasure Chest: A Teacher Advisory Source Book* published by NMSA (Hoversten, Doda, & Lounsbury, 1991). While it is not a curriculum per se, it provides information on how to start an advisory program as well as offers 120 specific advising activities. These activities may be organized into a three-year advising curriculum of 40 non-repeating activities organized by categories such as goal setting, getting to know oneself, and self-esteem, communication, feelings, friendship, peer pressure, communication, and group skills. *Middle School Advisement* by Ball (1996) provides activities that fall into one of three categories – life skills, study skills, and goal setting skills – for a one year program. Also included are some limited activities for multicultural awareness.

Preparation time invariably is an important consideration for teachers in selecting advisory activities. George and Alexander (1993) recommend that 20% of advisory time be devoted to activities that require little or no additional preparation but offer substantial positive outcomes. They offer a list of 20 such activities – student of the day/week, uninterrupted sustained silent reading, silent writing, academic advisory (a glorified study hall), career exploration (a series of career days with adults from the community), games, organization day (learning to schedule tests, projects, assignments, and other tasks for the week), videos, Magic Circle (an opportunity to talk about student concerns), current events, joke and riddle day, community help projects, intramurals, goal-setting day, holiday celebrations, schoolwide activity day (competitions among advisory groups), clubs, special meals, school help projects, and story time.

How do you evaluate an advisory program?

There is no one correct way to evaluate an advisory program, but evaluation will be particularly informative if the process and instruments selected are tailored to the specific program implemented. Program planners and evaluators should engage in both formative and summative evaluation of the program. Formative evaluation assesses the extent to which the necessary prerequisites for the program are in place, while summative evaluation is concerned with the actual effects of the advisory program. Once again, program emphasis becomes an important consideration.

If the program focuses on academic enhancement, for example, advisee outcome measures relevant to the academic content of the program such as percent of homework completed, reading comprehension/speed, and math achievement could be selected or constructed. Programs with a community emphasis might be concerned with changes in perceived levels of social support in the environment or changes in school climate. Research indicates that students who receive adequate support become better adjusted to middle school and have a more positive self-concept, lower feelings of depression, and greater liking of middle school (e.g., DuBois, Felner, Meares, & Krier, 1994; Dubois & Hirsch, 1990).

Given the community emphasis, assessment of both advisor and advisee perceptions is also essential. With Advocacy programs, evaluators might assess the degree to which advisees either confide in or perceive the advisor as a person to seek out for assistance with problems and the extent to which teachers and parents see the advisor as the person to contact regarding questions about the student. Regardless of program emphasis, valuable information can be derived from asking advisors and advisees about their satisfaction with and perceived effectiveness of the program, as well as inviting their suggestions for improving the program.

Table 2, on the following page, presents a list of some of the formative and summative evaluation issues or factors to consider in planning and evaluating an advisory program. The likelihood of a successful program is increased to the extent that each of the evaluation issues has been addressed. ▲

Table 2
Factors in evaluating an advisory program

1. The needs to be served by the program have been identified and agreed on by the major stakeholders.

2. Stakeholders have agreed that a stand-alone (i.e., separate period in the schedule) advisory is the best way to attempt to meet those needs.

3. Consensus about program emphases (goals) has been reached by the major stakeholders.

4. The program emphases appear reasonable given the time allotted for the program.

5. Activities have been selected that are relevant to program emphases.

6. A sufficient number of advisors are available to staff the type of program selected.

7. Advisors possess or have been trained in the needed advisory skills.

8. Advisors consistently implemented the selected activities.

9. The time set aside in the school schedule for advisory was consistently used for that purpose.

10. Suggestions that participants and stakeholders have for improving the program were solicited and reviewed.

11. Outcome measures (appropriate to the program emphases) have been selected and administered to the participants and to relevant stakeholders as appropriate.

12. Measures of satisfaction and perceived effectiveness of the program have been administered to the participants and to relevant stakeholders as appropriate.

Chapter IV
Directions

Advisory programs have been a fundamental, and, for the most part, unquestioned component of middle grades education since the beginning of the middle school movement. Moreover, its roots as an educational practice date back at least to the first decade of this century and the junior high school movement. Few practices, however, remain unchanged over time, and still fewer survive relatively intact if at all over a prolonged period. Rather, they tend to evolve to meet the perceived educational needs of the times. In this chapter, we discuss three possible new directions affecting advisory programs – changes in program emphases, middle school structural changes, and middle school curriculum changes. The first of these directions, program emphases, leaves the advisory concept and advisory programs intact and focuses on a simple change in the content or focus of those programs. The last two directions recognize the evolving nature of the middle school movement as well as the practical difficulties of effectively implementing freestanding advisory programs as they are currently constituted. The ultimate implication of these directions is eliminating freestanding programs and absorbing the advisory concept within mainstream middle grades education.

Changes in program emphases

One of the strengths of advisory has been its flexibility as a forum where the perceived needs of young adolescents and the social issues affecting them could be addressed. As different social issues emerged that affected the education and development of middle school students, advisory served as a vehicle where they could be discussed and where skills for coping with these issues could be acquired. Thus, as drugs increasingly affected middle school students, drug education components were incorporated into advisory programs. As violence increased in schools, conflict resolution curricula and peer mediation were added. As educators became more aware of the impact of racial, cultural, and other individual differences on education and society, efforts were made to emphasize appreciation of diversity during advisory.

> One of the strengths of advisory has been its flexibility as a forum where the perceived needs of young adolescents and the social issues affecting them could be addressed.

In the advisory typology we proposed, these issues – drugs, violence, diversity – fall under the skills (developmental guidance) emphasis. As society and the problems it poses becomes more complex, the life skills needed to cope with these problems also evolve and become more complex. Not surprisingly, some of the newer directions in advisory program content emphasize more global concepts rather than discrete skills, such as resisting drugs or avoiding conflicts. The Guilford County, North Carolina School System, for example, recently incorporated character education as one of the eight strands of its advisory program (*Stepping Up*, 1996). Activities in this strand revolve around such global concepts as fairness/justice, trustworthiness, citizenship, responsibility, and caring.

> Some of the newer directions in advisory program content emphasize more global concepts rather than discrete skills, such as resisting drugs or avoiding conflicts.

Not all support this developmental guidance emphasis. Kohn (1997), for example, criticizes character education (e.g., Lickona, 1991) as epitomizing the "fix-the-kid" approach to education.

What goes in the name of character education nowadays is often a collection of exhortations and extrinsic inducements designed to make children work harder and do what they're told....The point is to drill students in specific behaviors rather than to engage them in deep critical reflection about certain ways of being (Kohn, 1997, p. 429).

According to Kohn, a more effective approach to promoting social and moral development involves a balance of affective and cognitive concerns that is integrated into school life (see section following on curriculum changes), meets children's needs more effectively, and turns schools into caring communities. While his point is well taken, it is clear that attention to developing character in students is now widely advocated and usually leads to the use of specific activities. In addition to moral and character education, there are other ways the emphases of current advisory programs can be altered. For instance, Elias, Bruene-Butler, Blum, and Schulyer (1997) stress the importance of programs in social and emotional learning that are predicated on Goleman's emotional intelligence construct (Goleman, 1995). In these programs, students are taught social decision making and problem solving. As a general principle, it is likely that the emphases of future advisory programs will continue to reflect the nature of the societal and educational problems faced by middle school students and educators.

It is likely that the emphases of future advisory programs will continue to reflect the nature of the societal and educational problems faced by middle school students and educators.

Structural changes

While changes in program emphases leave the freestanding advisory concept intact and only alter the content or emphasis, merely changing emphases ignores many of the barriers and practical problems (see **Definitions** chapter) advisory programs impose on a middle school. Among these problems is the perceived artificiality of the program, the fact that it imposes a new structure on top of an already existing school structure.

In order to create an advisory period, the school schedule must be revamped to accommodate it. Teachers, likewise, have to be concerned about new preparations that might require the use of new and unfamiliar skills. Students, in some cases, are called upon to relate to a new adult not part of their previous school day. Parents must resolve the question of what this new and frequently non-academic period might contribute to their children's education when the quality of education and the rigor of academic programs provided by schools are being questioned. Because a freestanding advisory can pose significant practical problems for a middle school, several structural alternatives capable of achieving the same goals as current advisory programs may be considered.

A primary goal of many advisory programs is to create a climate of caring and community between teacher and students and in the school generally. A frequently related goal is to assist teachers in getting to know students well enough to become trusted advocates. Achieving both of these goals takes time. Moreover, advisory is not the only educational practice that facilitates attaining these goals. Student-teacher progression and multi-age grouping may also serve this purpose. Progression involves having the same students and the same team of teachers working together for two or more years. Multiage grouping results in students and teachers working together for more than one year, but increases the age range of the student community. By extending the amount of time that students and teachers spend together during the middle school years, both of these practices have the potential for fostering more enduring teacher-student relationships. The physical design of many modern middle schools has sixth, seventh, and eighth graders located in "houses" or "pods," which assists students in becoming more familiar with the same group of teachers and students as they progress from one grade level to the next. Familiarity fosters closer and more caring student-teacher and peer relationships as well as a stronger sense of community.

Another increasingly common practice in middle grades education is the use of two teacher teams, a practice that greatly reduces student-teacher ratio. Because the number of different students is reduced and those students spend at least two periods with each teacher, the relationships between the teachers and their students can often meet the expectations of the most successful advocacy and community AA programs. As a result, a separate advisory program may not even be needed in a two-teacher team arrangement.

Still other advisory alternatives have been suggested. For example, Vars (1989), a former core teacher, advocates using a variety of advising approaches based on the developmental level of students and the strengths of teachers. In fifth and sixth grades, it might best be carried out by the teacher in a self-contained classroom. This approach has the advantage of building on the strengths usually found in teachers trained for the elementary level. For seventh grade, Vars suggests that 20-30 minutes for advising might be added to the English-social studies or math-science block. This approach would necessitate a larger advisory load (50-60 students per teacher), but would be compensated for by the extended time the teacher and students spend together. Eighth grade advising would in such a situation involve a separate advisory period, but the advisors would also have their advisees in a regular class during the day. Some volunteer advisors could be drawn from elective classes and other areas to reduce the size of advisory groups, but every adult in the school would not be involved in the program for eighth graders. In addition to using different advisory approaches for different grade levels, Vars also proposes that not all teachers or teams at a particular grade level need use exactly the same approach. However, the use of these or other approaches are only temporary advising solutions as far as Vars is concerned. They are to be used only until middle school class sizes can be reduced substantially and until we are able to hire middle grade teachers broadly certified in and competent in guidance as well.

> In addition to using different advisory approaches for different grade levels, Vars proposes that not all teachers or teams at a particular grade level need use exactly the same approach.

Curriculum changes

The ultimate solution to the separate stand-alone problem will revolve around finding ways to integrate the caring, advising, guidance, and other desired advisory functions into the regular curriculum. This was done in the core curriculum that involved extensive student-teacher planning in a problem-centered block of time. It involved materials usually from English and social studies focused around life problems/interests taught by one teacher in an extended period of time.

The ultimate solution to the separate stand-alone problem will revolve around finding ways to integrate the caring, advising, guidance, and other desired advisory functions into the regular curriculum.

Beane (1990) first argued that the middle school reform movement has largely ignored the issue of curriculum reform. "Clearly, the major concern in middle level 'reform' has been on the organization of time and other institutional features rather than on the curriculum" (p. 18). If early adolescence represents a distinct developmental stage and if the middle school is to be based on issues of this stage, then he believes that the curriculum should be designed along developmentally appropriate lines and that it would look quite different from the academic, "special," and pseudo-vocational subjects we now have. He has proposed that the entire middle school curriculum focus on general education that he defines as the common needs, problems, interests, and concerns of young people and society. The curriculum would be composed of thematic units centered around the common personal and social (and societal) problems faced by all adolescents. Examples of the themes to be addressed in the curriculum are *transitions, identities, interdependence, social structures, wellness, living in the future, commercialism* and so forth. These themes would be explored by students using skills such as reflective thinking, problem solving, social action, as well as more traditional ones like mathematical and computational skills. However, the more traditional areas would be repositioned in the curriculum so that they are not isolated or self-justified but are addressed because of their functionality with respect to the particular theme under study. In addition, three key concepts – (a) democracy, (b) human dignity and the related ideas of freedom, equality, justice, and peace, and (c) cultural diversity that often influence current advisory programs – would permeate the curriculum (Beane, 1993).

Responses to Beane's proposal can be found in the work of other curriculum theorists who call for revision of the middle school curriculum. Proponents of inquiry approaches to instruction are among those who advocate for change and a rethinking of curriculum theory (e.g., Jacobsen, Eggen, & Kauchak, 1993). Inquiry methodology starts with a question or problem related to content. Students respond by proposing hypotheses, collecting data, pursuing the issue in individual and collaborative ways. Presumably students learn problem-solving techniques, learn how to gather and analyze information, distinguish fact from opinion, and explore ways to articulate their findings. Students are actively involved in their own learning and have the opportunity to pursue aspects of a problem that they find personally interesting. "By seeing how problems are solved in the classroom, they are provided with a model to follow in solving problems in other areas of their lives " (Jacobsen et al., 1993, p. 216).

The notion of interdisciplinary and integrated approaches to curriculum in the middle grades has been extended and clarified by Stevenson and Carr (1993) who distinguish multidisciplinary from integrated studies. Claiming as first priority "the developmental nature of the learners," the middle school studies they espouse were organized so that students' "ideas, interests and questions came first; prescribed content and skills were secondary" (p. 11). The goals of this integrated curriculum resemble those of some advisory programs: (a) students will grow more confident through relationships with and recognition by classmates and teachers, (b) students will work together cooperatively and have positive interpersonal relationships with peers and adults over an extended period of time, (c) students will develop social-ethical consciousness through service, exploration of beliefs and personal questions, decision making opportunities and (d) students will be challenged to think and construct understandings through enjoyable, hands-on activities and grow through experiences cultivated by prudent teachers and adult leaders.

A middle school curriculum that incorporated these goals in the manner proposed by Stevenson and Carr would clearly address adolescent needs through academic studies in a manner consistent with the recommendations of typical advisory programs. One example of a relevant integrated, interdisciplinary unit was presented by Bellavance and Girardin (1993). In this unit, reading, writing, health, and guidance curricula were built around the theme of self-study divided into four sections – identity, anatomy, sexuality and reproduction, and mental development of the brain. Students engaged in a variety of instructional activities including creating a newspaper, debating moral dilemmas, listening to guest speakers, and designing games about the operation of systems of the body. Although such proposals do have the potential for rendering current stand-alone advisory programs obsolete by absorbing their content into the general middle school curriculum, currently their status is clearly one of promise rather than payoff.

Conclusion

So where are we with respect to advisory programs, and what does the future hold for them? We have posed the thesis that an advisory program is just one route for achieving affective and other guidance goals of middle level education. From an historical perspective, freestanding advisory programs may end up as an interim (20th century) step in the development of middle school educational practices. Ultimately, the general success of advisory programs and the alternative middle grades educational practices that we have discussed will be determined by the results of experience and experimentation. At this time, neither the existing empirical nor the existing experiential data permit definitive conclusions about the outcomes of these practices.

There are some middle schools ready to move away from advisory programs in favor of integrating the affective with the cognitive. However, those schools just converting from the traditional junior high model or those who are still relatively new to the middle school experiment are likely to find that separate advisory programs are a way to meet important transitional, school climate, and student development goals. In that regard, we trust that the suggestions and conceptual framework provided in this publication will enable schools to improve the effectiveness of their advisory program. The comments of Trubowitz (1994) make a fitting closing statement.

> **...in the best of all educational worlds, advisories might not even be necessary. With small classes and with teacher recognition that the affective and cognitive are inextricably interrelated, what occurs in advisory programs can be made commonplace in regular classrooms. In the interim [effective] advisor-advisee programs can do much to enrich the school lives of young adolescents.** (p. 5) ▲

References

Alexander, W. M., & George, P.S. (1981). *The exemplary middle school.* New York: Holt, Rinehart, & Winston.

Alexander, W. M., Williams, E. L., Compton, M., Hines, V. A., & Prescott, D. (1968). *The emergent middle school.* New York: Holt, Rinehart and Winston, Inc.

Ames, N. L., & Miller, E. (1994). *Changing middle schools: How to make schools work for young adolescents.* San Francisco: Jossey Bass Publishers.

Aronson, D. (1997). The inside story. In F. Schulz (Ed.), *Multicultural education 97/98* (4th ed.) (pp. 138-143). Guilford, CT: Dushkin/McGraw-Hill.

Arnold, J. (1991, April). The revolution in middle school organization. *Momentum,* 20-25.

Ayres, L. R. (1994). Middle school advisory programs: Findings from the field. *Middle School Journal, 25* (3), 8-14.

Ball, T. (1996). *Middle school advisement.* Huntington Beach, CA: Teacher Created Materials, Inc.

Banks, J. A. (1994). *An introduction to multicultural education.* Boston: Allyn and Bacon.

Banks, J. A. (1995). Multicultural education and curriculum transformation. *Journal of Negro Education, 64,* 390-400.

Beane, J. A. (1990). *A middle school curriculum: From rhetoric to reality.* Columbus, OH: National Middle School Association.

Beane, J. A. (1993). *A middle school curriculum: From rhetoric to reality* (2nd ed.). Columbus, OH: National Middle School Association.

Bellavance, J., & Girardin, S. (1993). A self-study. In C. Stevenson and J. F. Carr (Eds.), *Integrated studies in the middle grades: "Dancing through walls."* (pp. 54-65). New York: Teachers College Press.

Bergmann, S., & Baxter, J. (1983). Building a guidance program and advisory concept for early adolescents. *NASSP Bulletin, 67* (463), 49-55.

Briggs, T. H. (1920). *The junior high school.* Boston: Houghton Mifflin Company.

Brooks, J. G., & Brooks, M. G. (1993). *The case for constructivist classrooms.* Alexandria: VA: Association for Supervision and Curriculum Development.

Burkhardt, R., & Fusco, E. (1990). *Advisory—An advocacy program for students.* Shoreham, NY: Shoreham-Wading River Middle School.

Bushnell, D., & George, P. S. (1993). Five crucial characteristics: Middle school teachers as effective advisers. *Schools in the Middle: Theory into Practice, 3* (1), 10-16.

Callahan, J. F. & Clark, L. H. (1988). *Teaching in the middle and secondary schools: Planning for competence.* New York: Macmillan Publishing Co.

Carnegie Council on Adolescent Development. (1989). *Turning points; Preparing American youth for the 21st century.* New York: Carnegie Corporation.

Cawelti, G. (1988, November). Middle schools a better match with early adolescent needs, ASCD survey finds. *ASCD Curriculum Update,* pp. 1-12 .

Cole, C. G. (1981). *Guidance in middle level schools: Everyone's responsibility.* Columbus, OH: National Middle School Association.

Cole, C. G. (1994). Teachers' attitudes before beginning a teacher advisory program. *Middle School Journal, 25* (5), 3-7.

Commission on Minority Participation in Education and American Life. (1988). *One-third of a nation.* Washington, DC: The American Council on Education.

Connors, N. A. (1986). *A case study to determine the essential components and effects of an advisor/advisee program in an exemplary middle school.* Unpublished doctoral dissertation, Florida State University, Tallahassee, FL.

Cremin, L. (1961). *The transformation of the school: Progressivism in American education, 1876-1957.* New York: Alfred A. Knopf.

DuBois, D. L., & Hirsch, B. J. (1990). School and neighborhood friendships of Blacks and Whites in early adolescence. *Child Development, 62,* 524-536.

DuBois, D. L., Felner, R. D., Meares, H., & Krier, M. (1994). Prospective investigation of the effects of socioeconomic disadvantage, life stress, and social support on early adolescent adjustment. *Journal of Abnormal Psychology, 103*, 511-522.

Eccles, J. S., Wigfield, A., Midgley, C., Reuman, D., Mac Iver, D., & Feldlaufer, H. (1993). Negative effects of traditional middle schools on students' motivation. *The Elementary School Journal, 93*, 555-559.

Elias, M. J., Bruene-Butler, L., Blum, L., & Schulyer, T. (1997). How to launch a social and emotional learning program. *Educational Leadership, 54* (8), 15-19.

Epstein, J. L., & Mac Iver, D. J. (1990). *Education in the middle grades: Overview of national practices and trends*. Columbus, OH: National Middle School Association.

Erb, T. O. (1993). Responding to giftedness in middle schools: Instruction for the information age. *North Carolina Association for Supervision and Curriculum Development Journal*, Winter, 27.

Espe, L. (1993). The effectiveness of teacher advisors in a junior high. *The Canadian School Executive, 12* (7), 15-19.

Galassi, J. P., & Gulledge, S. A. (1997). The middle school counselor and teacher-advisor programs. *The School Counselor*,

Galassi, J. P., Gulledge, S. A., & Cox, N. D. (1997a). Middle school advisories: Retrospect and prospect. *Review of Educational Research*,

Galassi, J. P., Gulledge, S. A., & Cox, N. D. (1997b). Planning and maintaining sound advisory programs. *Middle School Journal, 28* (5), 35-41.

Gay, G. (1994). Coming of age ethnically: Teaching young adolescents of color. *Theory Into Practice. 33*, 149-155.

Gay, G. (1997). Bridging multicultural theory and practice. In F. Schulz (Ed.), *Multicultural education 97/98* (4th ed.) (pp. 109-113). Guilford, CT: Dushkin/McGraw-Hill.

George, P. S., & Alexander, W. M. (1993). *The exemplary middle school* (2nd ed.). Orlando, FL: Harcourt Brace College Publishers.

George, P. S., & Bushnell, D. (1993). What works and why? The key to successful advisement activities. *Schools in the Middle: Theory into Practice, 3* (1), 3,9.

George, P. S., & Lawrence, G. (1982). *Handbook for middle school teaching*. Glenview, Illinois: Scott, Foresman, and Co.

George, P. S., & Oldaker, L. L. (1985). *Evidence for the middle school*. Columbus, OH: National Middle School Association.

George, P. S., Stevenson, C., Thomason, J., & Beane, J. (1992). *The middle school and beyond*. Alexandria, Virginia: Association for Supervision and Curriculum Development.

Gill, J., & Read, J. E. (1990). The "experts" comment on adviser-advisee programs. *Middle School Journal, 21* (5), 31-33.

Glasser, W. (1992). *The quality school: Managing students without coercion* (2nd ed.). NY: Harper Perennial.

Goldberg, M. F. (1977). House group: A guidance role for the teacher. *NASSP Bulletin, 61* (410), 61-64.

Goleman, D. (1995). *Emotional intelligence*. New York: Bantam Books.

Guilford County School System. (1996). *Stepping up to success with the Guilford County advisory program.*. Greensboro, NC: Author.

Gysbers, N. C., & Henderson, P. (1994). *Developing and managing your school guidance program* (2nd ed.). Alexandria, VA: American Counseling Association.

Havighurst, R. J. (1972). *Developmental tasks and education* (3rd ed.). New York: David McKay.

Henderson, P., & La Forge, J. (1989). The role of the middle school counselor in teacher-advisor programs. *The School Counselor, 36*, 348-351.

Hertzog, C. J. (1992). Middle level advisory programs: From the ground up. *Schools in the Middle, 2* (1), 23-27.

Hieronimus, N. C. (1917). The teacher-advisor in the junior high school. *Educational Administration and Supervision, 3*, 91-95..

Hoversten, C., Doda, N., & Lounsbury, J. (1991). *Treasure chest: A teacher advisory source book*. Columbus, OH: National Middle School Association.

Hutcheson, J., & Moeller, T. E. (1995). Using evaluation to recreate a middle level teacher education program. *Middle School Journal, 26* (5), 32-36.

Jacobsen, D., Eggen, P., & Kauchak, D. (1993). *Methods for teaching: A skills approach* (4th ed.). New York: Macmillan.

Jenkins, J. M. (1977). The teacher-adviser: An old solution looking for a problem. *NASSP Bulletin, 61* (410), 29-34.

Johnson, R. L., & Salmon, S. J. (1979). Caring and counseling: Shared tasks in advisement schools. *Personnel and Guidance Journal, 57,* 474-477.

Kaplan, L. S. (1997). Parents' rights: Are school counselors at risk? *The School Counselor, 44,* 334-343.

Kohn, A. (1997). How not to teach values: A critical look at character education. *Phi Delta Kappan, 78,* 429-439.

Ladson-Billings, G. (1994). *Dreamkeepers: Succesful teachers of African-American children.* San Francisco, CA: Jossey-Bass.

Lewis, A. C. (1991). *Gaining ground: The highs and lows of urban middle school reform 1989-1991.* New York: The Edna McConnell Clark Foundation.

Lickona, T. (1991). *Educating for character: How our schools can teach respect and responsibility.* New York: Bantam Books.

Mac Iver, D. J., & Epstein, E. J. (1991). Responsive practices in the middle grades: Teacher teams, advisory groups, remedial instruction, and school transition programs. *American Journal of Education, 99,* 587-622.

McEwin, C. K. (1981). Establishing teacher-advisory programs in middle level schools. *Journal of Early Adolescence, 1,* 337-348.

McEwin, C. K., Dickinson, T. S., & Jenkins, D. M. (1996). *America's middle schools: Practices and progress—A 25 year perspective.* Columbus, OH: National Middle School Association.

Meece, J. L. (1997). *Child and adolescent development for educators.* New York: Mc Graw-Hill Co., Inc.

Muth, K. D., & Alvermann, D. E. (1992). *Teaching and learning in the middle grades.* Boston: Allyn and Bacon.

Myrick, R. D. (1987). TAP: Key to developmental guidance. *International Quarterly, 5* (4), 24-29.

Myrick, R. D. (1993). *Developmental guidance and counseling: A practical approach* (2nd ed.). Minneapolis, MN: Educational Media Corporation.

Myrick, R. D., Highland, M., & Highland, W. (1986). Preparing teachers to be advisors. *Middle School Journal, 17* (3), 15-16.

Myrick, R. D., & Myrick, L. S. (1990). *The teacher advisor program.* Ann Arbor, MI: ERIC/CAPS.

National Association of Secondary School Principals. (1985). *An agenda for excellence at the middle level.* Reston, VA: Author.

National Middle School Association. (1982-1992). *This we believe.* Columbus, OH: Author.

National Middle School Association. (1995). *This we believe: Developmentally responsive middle level schools.* Columbus, OH: Author.

North Carolina Department of Public Instruction (NCDPI), (1991). *Middle grades task force report, Last best chance.* Raleigh, NC.: Carnegie Middle Grade School State Policy Initiative, N.C.D.P.I.

O'Neil, J. (1997). Why are all the black kids sitting together? *Educational Leadership, 65* (4), 12-17.

Pallas, A. M., Natriello, G., & McDill, E. L. (1989). The changing nature of the disadvantaged population: Current dimensions and future trends. *Educational Researcher, 18* (5), 16-22.

Putbrese, L. (1989). Advisory programs at the middle level - The students' response. *NASSP Bulletin, 73,* 111-115. .

Rice, F. P. (1998). *Human development: A life span approach* (3rd ed.). Upper Saddle River, New Jersey: Prentice Hall.

Roberts, L. R., Sarigiani, P. A., Petersen, A. C., & Newman, J. L. (1990). Gender differences in the relationship between achievement and self-image during early adolescence. *Journal of Early Adolescence, 10,* 159-175.

Sarasota County School System. (1985). *PRIME TIME activities handbook.* Sarasota, FL: Author.

Sardo-Brown, D., & Shetlar, J. (1994). Listening to students and teachers to revise a rural advisory program. *Middle School Journal, 26* (1), 23-25.

Scales, P. C., & McEwin, C. K. (1994). *Growing pains: The making of America's middle school teachers.* National Middle School Association.

School Board of Alachua County. *(1984). FAME: Finding acceptance in the middle school environment: Grade 7.* Gainesville, FL: Author.

Slonim, M. (1991). *Children, culture, and ethnicity.* New York: Garland.

Spring, J. (1995). *The intersection of cultures: Multicultural education in the United States.* New York: McGraw-Hill, Inc.

Stevenson, C. (1992). *Teaching ten to fourteen year olds.* New York: Longman Publishing Co.

Stevenson, C., & Carr, J. (1993). *Integrated studies in the middle grades: "Dancing through walls."* New York: Teachers College Press.

Swick, K. J., Boutte, G., & Van Scoy, I. (1997). Families and schools building multicultural values together. In F. Schulz (Ed.), *Multicultural education 97/98* (4th ed.) (pp. 116-120). Guilford, CT: Dushkin/McGraw-Hill.

Tatum, B. D. (1997). *"Why are all the black kids sitting together in the cafeteria?" and other conversations about race.* New York: Basic books.

Totten, S., & Nielson, W. (1994). Middle level students' perceptions of their advisor/advisee program: A preliminary study. *Current issues in middle level education. 3* (2), 8-33.

Trubowitz, S. (1994). The quest for the good advisor-advisee program. *Middle Ground,* Winter, 3-5.

Valentine, J. W., Clark, D. C., Irvin, J. L., Keefe, J. W., & Melton, G. (1993) *Leadership in middle level education Volume 1: A national survey of middle level leaders and schools.* Reston, VA: National Association of Secondary School Principals.

Van Hoose, J. (1991). The ultimate goal: AA across the day. *Midpoints, 2* (1), 1-7.

Van Til, W., Vars, G. F., & Lounsbury, J. H. (1961). *Modern education for the junior high school years.* Indianapolis, IN: The Bobbs-Merrill Company, Inc.

Vars, G. F. (1989). Getting closer to middle level students: Options for teacher-adviser guidance programs. *Schools in the Middle: A report on trends and practices.* Reston, VA: National Association of Secondary School Principals.

Vermont Association for Middle Level Education and the Vermont Department of Education. (1996). *Partner Teaming* (Videotape). Montpelier, VT: Author.

Wardle, F. (1997). Proposal: An antibias and ecological model for multicultural education. In F. Schulz (Ed.), *Multicultural education 97/98* (4th ed.) (pp. 150-154). Guilford, CT: Dushkin/McGraw-Hill.

Watson, C. R. (1997). *Middle school case studies: Challenges, perceptions, and practices.* New Jersey: Prentice-Hall.

White, G. P., & Greenwood, S. C. (1991). Study skills and the middle level adviser/advisee program. *NASSP Bulletin 75* (537), 88-94.

Wittmer, J. (1993). Developmental school guidance and counseling: Its history and reconceptualization. In J. Wittmer (Ed.), *Managing your school counseling program: K-12 developmental strategies* (pp. 2-11). Minneapolis, MN: Educational Media Corporation.

Wittmer, J., & Myrick, R. D. (1989). *The teacher as facilitator.* Minneapolis, MN: Educational Media Corporation.

Ziegler, S., & Mulhall, L. (1994). Establishing and evaluating a successful advisory program in a middle school. *Middle School Journal, 25* (4), 42-46.

APPENDIX
Advisory Descriptor Cards

Advocacy

1	7	13	19
Engage in informal one-to-one conversations/conferences with the advisor	Experience a one-to-one relationship with the advisor which is characterized by warmth, concern, openness, and understanding	Have a "special relationship" with the advisor in which the student can discuss any and all concerns—academic, personal, and social	Have an advisor who serves as the student's advocate with teachers, parents, etc.

Community

2	8	14	20
Participate in activities to build group spirit/cohesiveness and a sense that the advisory group is special	Experience the advisory group as a "home place" or a "family" within the school	Work together on a common project to benefit the advisory group, the school, the community, etc.	Support and be supported by other advisory group members in discussing/facing common problems and concerns of growing up

Skills (Developmental Guidance)

3	9	15	21
Learn problem-solving and/or decision-making skills	Learn to understand and appreciate people who are different from themselves	Learn how to resist pressure to use drugs or to engage in other self-destructive behaviors	Learn about careers, career development, and life planning

Invigoration

4	10	16	22
Participate in nonacademic activities that are fun and "recharge one's batteries" prior to resuming instruction	Participate in intramural sports	Participate in clubs and hobbies	Celebrate birthdays and special occasions

Academic

5	11	17	23
Learn/practice study skills and goal setting	Read for enrichment or personal interest	Do creative or journal writing	Complete homework or receive tutoring or other type of additional academic instruction.

Administrative

6	12	18	24
Receive school announcements or other materials	Review school policies and procedures	Turn in money for trips and special events	Complete miscellaneous "housekeeping" activities such as filling out forms, requested information, etc.

Using a card-sorting activity to set priorities for your advisory program

1. The first pile of four cards should contain the statements that are the most important or the highest priority for your advisory program.

2. The second pile of four cards should contain the next most important or the next highest priority statements.

3. The third pile of cards should contain statements of the lowest priority and should contain the remaining sixteen cards.

4. Once you have completed your sorting, write the numbers of the cards you placed in piles one and two (highest and next highest priority) on the Summary Card under the "highest" and "next highest" categories.

5. Return the summary card and all the other cards to the person who is facilitating this exercise.

6. Refer to a fuller explanation (beginning on page 36) for interpreting the choices made and their implications for your advisory program.

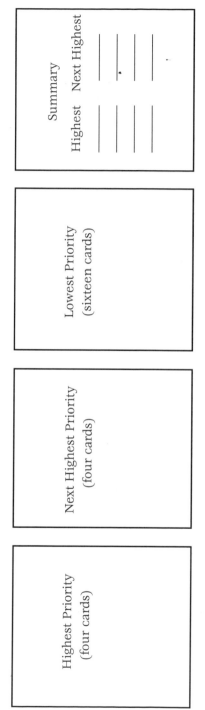

Highest Priority
(four cards)

Next Highest Priority
(four cards)

Lowest Priority
(sixteen cards)

Summary

Highest   Next Highest

National Middle School Association

National Middle School Association was established in 1973 to serve as a voice for professionals and others interested in the education of young adolescents. The association has grown rapidly and now enrolls members in all fifty states, the Canadian provinces, and forty-two other nations. In addition, fifty-six state, regional, and provincial middle school associations are official affiliates of NMSA.

NMSA is the only association dedicated exclusively to the education, development, and growth of young adolescents. Membership is open to all. While middle level teachers and administrators make up the bulk of the membership, central office personnel, college and university faculty, state department officials, other professionals, parents, and lay citizens are members and active in supporting our single mission – improving the educational experiences of 10-15 year olds. This open and diverse membership is a particular strength of NMSA.

The association provides a variety of services, conferences, and materials in fulfilling its mission. The association publishes *Middle School Journal*, the movement's premier professional journal; *Research in Middle Level Education Quarterly*; *Middle Ground, the Magazine of Middle Level Education; Target*, the association's newsletter; and *Family Connection*, a newsletter for families. In addition, the association publishes more than sixty books and monographs on all aspects of middle level education. The association's highly acclaimed annual conference, which has drawn approximately 10,000 registrants in recent years, is held in the fall.

For information about NMSA and its many services contact headquarters at 4151 Executive Parkway, Suite 300, Westerville, Ohio 43081, TELEPHONE: 800 528-NMSA; FAX: 614-895-4750; WWW.NMSA.ORG